AN ORGANIC HANDBOOK

Managing Soil

without using chemicals

Jo Readman

the organic
organisation

HDRA/Search Press

Published in Great Britain 2004

Search Press Ltd
Wellwood, North Farm Road,
Tunbridge Wells, Kent TN2 3DR

in association with

HDRA
Ryton Organic Gardens
Coventry CV8 3LG

Originally published as *Soil Care and Management* in 1991
by Search Press Ltd

Illustrations by Polly Pinder
Photographs by Charlotte de la Bédoyère

The author would like to thank: Mike Hodgson of the Soil
Survey and Land Research Centre for his technical editing
of the book; Dave Readman for helping to type the
manuscript; HDRA for their support.

The publishers would like to thank: The Sussex Botanical
Recording Society for their assistance and for permission
to reproduce the photographs of coltsfoot (Pat Donovan)
and corn spurrey (John Fisher) on page 11; Jo Readman
for the photograph of horsetail on page 11; HDRA for the
photograph of a crop rotation on page 32.

ISBN 1 84448 011 9

Printed in Malaysia by Times Offset (M) Sdn Bhd

Conversion Chart

From centimetres to inches		*From grammes to ounces*	
1 cm	= ½ in	7 g =	¼ oz
2.5 cm	= 1 in	14 g =	½ oz
5 cm	= 2 in	28 g =	1 oz
10 cm	= 4 in	110 g =	4 oz
50 cm	= 20 in	450 g =	16 oz (1 lb)
100 cm (1 m)	= 40 in	*From litres to pints*	
1 sq m	= 1.2 sq yds	1 l = 1.75 pt	

Exact conversions from imperial to metric
measures are not possible, so the metric
measures have been rounded up.

Introduction

Healthy soil is the basis of a fertile, productive garden. However, many of us have to cope with soils that are far from perfect. You may have a heavy clay that no amount of digging will lighten or, at the other extreme, a soil which is more like seaside sand. With a little care and attention all soils are capable of producing healthy plants of suitable species.

The soil skeleton is composed of mineral particles formed over thousands of years from the breakdown of rocks. However, a true living soil only starts to form when the soil life moves in. These creatures, such as worms and bacteria, work together to provide the ideal conditions for plant growth. The plant roots in your garden need to grow down through, and anchor in, the soil in order to live, breathe, and take up water and nutrients all at the same time! Soil organisms recycle plant and animal waste (organic matter) to provide plant food. With the help of this organic matter they also structure the soil to provide well-designed living quarters for the roots and themselves, with room for water, air and growth.

Nature seems to have it all set up, so why do you need to manage the soil? You may wish to grow a wider range of plants in your garden than nature ever intended on a particular soil type. You may also have disturbed the soil and removed nutrients when cropping for food or trimming your ornamentals and lawns. Many gardeners try to overcome this problem by feeding the plants with artificial fertiliser and accept the task on most soils of looking after soil structure. The organic gardener feeds the soil life, recycling organic matter. This leads to a healthy work force under your feet, a healthy soil and healthy plants.

Whatever the size of your garden and state of your soil, this book contains information to help you get to know and work with it. The first section looks at the vital soil life, the basis of a good organic garden. The book then examines the soil, what it is made of, what type it is, and how it 'works', and shows ways in which you can analyse it. Then comes the all-important part – soil management. This covers how to look after your soil and improve it, once you know what type you are dealing with. Finally, there is a section on trouble shooting – some answers for those problem soils. Soil deserves to be treated with care and respect as it is our greatest garden asset.

The living soil

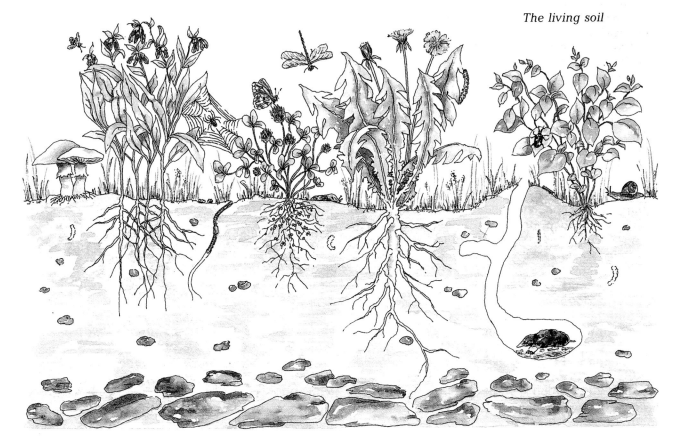

SOIL MATTERS

Soil life

Getting to know your allies

Before you feed your underground helpers, you have to get to know them. The weight of soil life in the top 30 cm of a fertile garden is about 700g/sq m!

The ever friendly earthworm
The star of the soil world must be the worm. These creatures eat mineral and organic matter which they grind up in their gut. As the worm digs through the soil it leaves channels which increase soil aeration and drainage, and encourage deep rooting. Every day, worms produce their own weight in worm-casts which are highly fertile, containing more nitrogen, phosphorus, potassium, magnesium and calcium than the surrounding soil. The casts, shaped in a walnut-like coil, are held together by gums and lime, improving the soil structure. The calcium that they contain even encourages a bacteria that secretes vitamin B12, a natural chemical that has been shown to improve crop yields. Earthworms can process 6 mm of soil annually, and a 1000 m^2 garden plot can support about 25,000 worms with 4.5 km of tunnels in the top 30 cm. People have always had a high regard for worms. Aristotle called them the intestines of the earth. To encourage worms in your garden:
- aim for a soil pH of 6.5
- add plenty of organic matter in spring and autumn
- keep them warm in winter with a mulch
- keep cultivation to a minimum in autumn and spring when worms are active in the top 15 cm

size ×2

The voracious hunters, the ground beetles
Some soil organisms recycle food by eating pests. Ground beetles and rove beetles are nocturnal prowlers, but you may be lucky enough to see one during the day when shifting compost or moving stones because this is where they find their prey — the slug. To encourage these creatures a lot of

ground cover is required. Also, try not to squash their larvae: they may look like pests but are voracious carnivores. Watch for the ground beetles with chestnut coloured legs, however, as they have a passion for strawberries.

Of course, there are many more soil organisms than the ones picked out here, ranging from those with a single cell to large burrowing mammals, such as rabbits, mice and moles. Even the pesky moles have some advantages as the hills they throw up make beautiful compost for seedlings when mixed with leaf mould and worm-casts.

If you want to find out more about your small soil life, then try setting up a trap, such as a jar, hollow potato or carrot, sunk into the ground. The table overleaf should help you discover whether you have caught a friend or foe.

size ×5

The springing springtails

Another important soil creature is a primitive wingless insect, the springtail. Do not be afraid if, when handling soil or compost, you find these little browny-grey creatures leaping into the air. They recycle vegetable matter and when disturbed escape by releasing a spring under their bodies.

The invisible inhabitants

Mention of bacteria and fungi all too often conjures up images of death and diseases such as scab, blight and club root. However, most soil bacteria and fungi are essential for a healthy soil. The microbes, as their name suggests, are very small. A quarter of a million could sit comfortably on the full stop at the end of this sentence. There is certainly strength in numbers. In a teaspoon of soil you will find more microbes than there are people on the planet! Although you cannot see them, you may be able to smell them. One microbe, the actinomycete, which decomposes organic matter,

helps to give the soil its smell of sweet earth. Many soil bacteria recycle organic matter and some are coated with a sugary gum which helps stick the soil into crumbs. Others, as shown on page 8, can make nitrogen fertiliser. Fungi, too, have many tricks up their hyphae. Some eat wood and others recycle food even in acid soils. The prize for ingenuity should go to the fungi with the cowboy tactics: they make nooses out of their thread-like bodies to catch and strangle nematode worms (soil pests). One group of fungi, the mycorrhizas, form an intimate relationship with plant roots, helping them absorb water and nutrients, protecting them from disease and boosting their growth by secretion of natural growth hormones. In return, the plant feeds them with sugar.

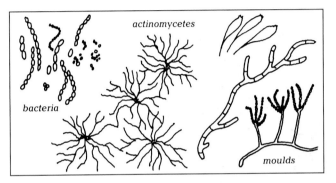

You can encourage beneficial microbes by applying, you've guessed it, well-rotted organic matter and keeping your nose to the ground for the sweet smell of success.

Plant roots

Plants are one of the most important parts of soil life. Most have roots which anchor the plant in the soil and take up water and food through root hairs, tiny tube-like extensions behind the root tip. Plant roots are essential in a living soil as they:

● split rocks, helping soil formation

● give out chemicals, helping dissolve soil minerals to feed the plant

● add to the organic matter when they die

● bind soil particles together

● leave channels for air and water

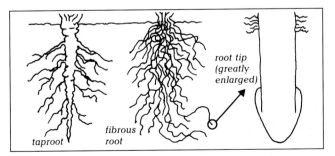

Friend or foe

	Name	Friend	Foe	Comments
	Earthworms	√		Recycle nutrients. Help soil structure.
	Potworms	√		Recycle nutrients. Indicate high levels of wet or acidic organic matter.
	Nematodes	√√	√	Recycle nutrients. Some are predators and some pests.
	Slugs and snails	√	√	Devour garden plants and decaying matter.
	Ground beetles	√		Eat pests.
	Beetle larvae	√	√	Some species eat pests, others damage crops, e.g. wireworm.
	Cutworms		√	Larvae feed at soil level, severing plant roots.
	Fly larvae	√	√	Recycle nutrients. Some are pests, e.g. carrot root.
	Springtails	√		Recycle nutrients.
	Symphyla	√√	√	Recycle nutrients. Some eat seedlings.
	Bristletails	√		Recycle nutrients.
	Protura	√		Recycle nutrients.
	Ants	√	√	Structure soil. Also spread seeds, nest in plant roots and can increase aphid populations.
	Woodlice	√	√	Recycle nutrients, even if they are in a strawberry!
	Centipedes	√		Eat pests.
	Millipedes	√	√	Recycle nutrients. Eat crop root of some plants.
	Spiders	√		Eat pests.
	Mites	√	√	Recycle nutrients. Eat pests and beneficial organisms. Some species attack crops.
	False scorpions	√		Recycle nutrients. Eat pests.
	Bacteria and fungi	√√	√	Recycle nutrients. Structure soils. Some types spread disease.

Cycles in your garden

Soil life, plants and animals do not work in isolation but form a living cycle in your garden. The soil life feed the plants, the plants feed you, and to complete the picture you feed the soil. Two important elements that are cycled through the soil, plant and animal are carbon and nitrogen.

The carbon cycle

Life is built on a framework of carbon. Plants photosynthesize, that is, they make carbon compounds (sugar) from water and carbon dioxide in the air using the sun's energy. The only waste product is oxygen. How clean! The carbon is recycled through plants, animals, bacteria and fungi and eventually returns to the air as carbon dioxide. The carbon compounds can be used for:

● *respiration* – most organisms use oxygen to break up the sugar, to release energy for living and growing

● *growth* – built up into plant, animal and microbe tissue

● *organic matter* – when living tissue dies and decays

The carbon cycle

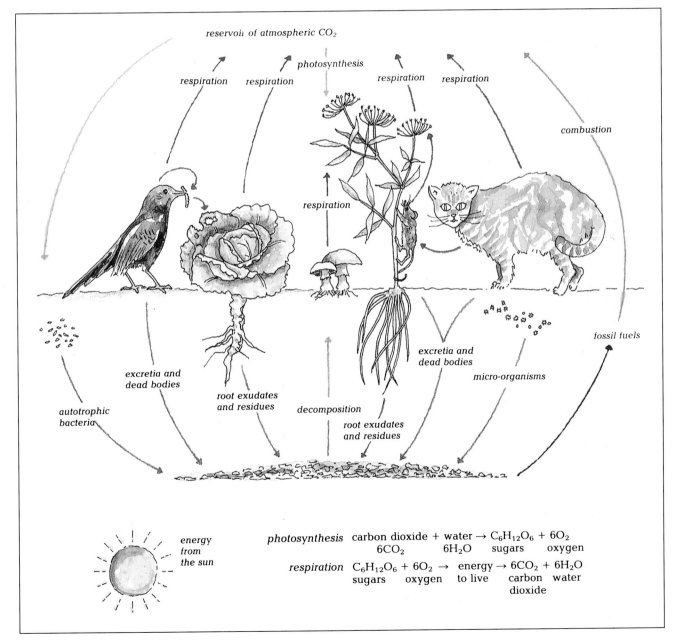

energy from the sun

photosynthesis carbon dioxide + water → $C_6H_{12}O_6$ + $6O_2$
$6CO_2$ $6H_2O$ sugars   oxygen

respiration $C_6H_{12}O_6$ + $6O_2$ → energy → $6CO_2$ + $6H_2O$
sugars   oxygen   to live   carbon   water
            dioxide

Labels in figure: reservoir of atmospheric CO_2; respiration; respiration; photosynthesis; respiration; respiration; combustion; respiration; excretia and dead bodies; root exudates and residues; decomposition; root exudates and residues; excretia and dead bodies; micro-organisms; fossil fuels; autotrophic bacteria

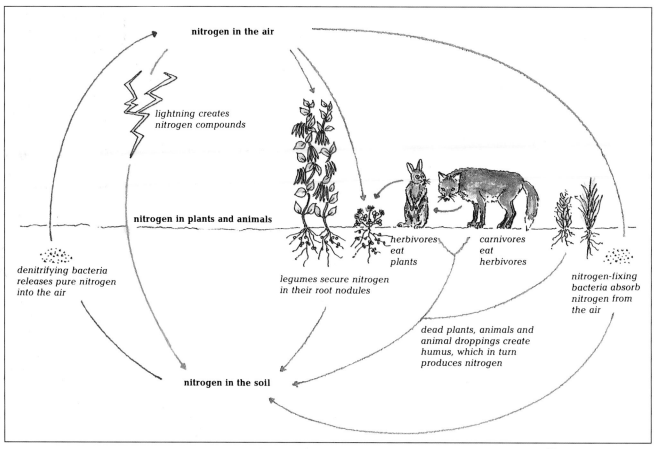

The nitrogen cycle

Labels in diagram:
- nitrogen in the air
- lightning creates nitrogen compounds
- nitrogen in plants and animals
- denitrifying bacteria releases pure nitrogen into the air
- legumes secure nitrogen in their root nodules
- herbivores eat plants
- carnivores eat herbivores
- nitrogen-fixing bacteria absorb nitrogen from the air
- dead plants, animals and animal droppings create humus, which in turn produces nitrogen
- nitrogen in the soil

The nitrogen cycle

Nitrogen, too, is cycled through living organisms which make it into protein by joining it to carbon compounds. The air is 78% nitrogen but plants cannot use it in this form, and need to take it up as 'nitrate' through their roots. Chemical gardeners apply nitrate from a bag. Organic gardeners encourage the soil life to do the work. The nitrogen-fixing bacteria are the cornerstone of all life and turn nitrogen gas into body protein. Legumes, plants of the pea and bean family, have these bacteria in their roots and pay for their protein supper by providing rent-free accommodation, raw materials and energy in the form of sugar.

With peas and beans in the vegetable patch, lupins and sweet peas in the flower beds, clover on the lawns and green manures (such as tares and lupins), you can 'fix' nitrogen all over your garden. Other nitrogen fixers, such as the bacteria azotobacter, are found free-living in our soils and compost.

Many other types of bacteria are important in the nitrogen cycle. Some need protein just like we do. They make it from organic matter. If the material is stemmy, e.g. straw, then the bacteria need to eat extra nitrogen. They take this from the soil and can steal a plant's supply. To avoid this, you can compost stemmy material and add materials high in nitrogen (see page 36). When you add such well-rotted compost to your garden, these particular bacteria will have already made their protein. When they die, other bacteria change the protein into nitrate plant food.

HELP FOR THE HELPERS
To keep the garden cycles going you should:
- add organic matter at the right times for your helpers' to live in and on
- make compost to give the soil life and plants a balanced diet
- encourage a good soil structure
- make sure there is enough air and water in the soil
- make sure you have the right pH
- grow lots of different plants, including legumes
- keep the ground covered
- keep the soil warm; soil life works best above 6°C

What is soil?

The word soil has many different meanings. Some think of it as a material in which plants grow, which provides them with nutrients and physical support. We know now that it is far more than that. It is a home for the soil life which can supply plants with nearly all their needs. The garden soil is a very complex structure and all these parts are organised and work together. Not all soils have the same proportions and not all soils are the same type. They may be heavy or light, wet or dry, acid or alkaline. Each type has its advantages and disadvantages.

Soils are made up of many parts. Half of the volume of a lump of good soil is usually made up of mineral matter from weathered rock, and organic matter from plants and animals. Then come the all-important soil dwellers. The rest is made up of air and water which is found in pores between the particles. The proportions of air and water vary considerably, both from soil to soil and with the season, but both are vital to a healthy soil.

The first step is getting to know your soils. What are they made of? What plants will grow best in them? You can plan how to manage your soils in order to get the most out of them. This involves creating the ideal conditions for the soil life and plant roots.

Getting to know your soil – on the surface

Whether taking over a new garden or allotment, or venturing out to create a beautiful, productive organic garden, the first step is to find out what your soil is like. The existing plants can tell you a great deal about the health and state of your soil without you even reaching for a trowel or spade.

Nettle
Nettles indicate a nitrogenous, fertile soil which has plenty of iron. Nettles show that a soil may have been overmanured. They are often found on the sites of old garden privies or compost heaps and the soil beneath them is rich and full of humus.

Chickweed
Dense clumps of chickweed are also indicators of soils with a high nutrient and humus content. As you clear these annuals from your seedbed, greenhouse and vegetable plots, console yourself with the fact that your soil is fertile.

Nettle

Chickweed

Vetch

The vetch family are legumes, and, as they fix their own nitrogen, they can survive in soils that are low in this nutrient. They may, therefore, indicate poor fertility. You can grow some vetches, such as winter tares, as green manures and incorporate them to build up the soil fertility, enabling other crops to grow successfully.

Medick

Medick is another legume that may indicate a soil low in nitrogen, particularly when it spreads with clovers on the lawn.

Azalea

If you find healthy azaleas, rhododendrons, camellias and heathers in your new garden, then you probably have an acid soil. However, take a close look to make sure that the previous gardener has not sunk them into peat beds to keep the pH in that area down.

Pink (dianthus)

These beautiful fragrant plants prefer and grow best in a slightly alkaline, well-drained soil. I have seen one on an acid sandy soil but it looked far from vigorous!

Rock rose

This tough little plant with delicate paper-thin flowers survives well on dry sandy soils. (This picture was taken in autumn, showing the plant's seed-pods.) Other plants on the same site may need more organic matter in order to grow well.

Corn spurrey

If, in addition to azaleas, you find this weed in the garden, then the soil is definitely acidic. Corn spurrey is common on poor sandy soils and will thrive where the pH is as low as 4, where most crops would perish.

Astilbe

Astilbes require a permanently moist soil to survive. If they look healthy, even in the middle of summer, then you can be sure that the soil beneath them contains a lot of moisture.

Coltsfoot

In a neglected garden, coltsfoot is an excellent indicator of heavy soil. Its yellow dandelion-like flowers in spring will show you that the soil beneath may need aeration.

Horsetail

This primitive weed, the horsetail, is an indicator of a wet soil and needs moisture all year round. If you go round the garden on a hot, sunny day and see horsetails, then it is possible that in the winter months the soil will become cold and waterlogged.

Thyme

This fragrant little plant is an indicator of dry, free-draining soil and also prefers neutral or limy ground. I have tried to grow it on heavy soils for years, with little success, and was most put out to see it spreading like a weed in the arid interior of Spain.

11

The soil profile

Although the surface of the soil can tell you a great deal, you will benefit by going underground. Soil is made up of different layers, all of which play an important part in plant growth. Looking at the sequence of these layers, called a soil profile, will give you many clues about how to manage your soils. Profiles can show you defects in the soil, depth of the soil, type of bedrock, drainage characteristics, type of structure and moisture-holding capacity.

GENERAL PROFILE

There are three main kinds of soil layer or horizon, A, B and C, corresponding to the topsoil, subsoil and deep subsoil.

A
- Can be arable, pasture, woodland, garden, etc.
- Where plant roots feed and most soil life is found.
- Rich in organic matter and dark in colour.
- In the UK it ranges from 5 cm to 60 cm or more in old, deeply worked gardens.
- In natural sites there is often a layer of undecomposed organic matter on the surface.

B
- Contains fewer roots and less soil life.
- Important in drainage.
- Soil particles arranged in bigger clumps – aggregates.
- Clays and other minerals, such as iron and aluminium oxides, can accumulate here.

C
- Weathered rock and parent material.
- Varies in composition.
- May be found at shallow depth, particularly on high ground or steep slopes.
- Formed from one of many types of rock, such as limestone, granite or sandstone, or from ice age drift or recent alluvial deposits.
- Most UK soils are not straight from rock.

How to dig a profile

You need an area of approximately 1 sq m in order to dig a profile. Choose a typical site away from trees and buildings. You need a plastic sheet on which to place the layers as you remove them because they need to go back in the right order. Remove the turf or surface layer, then the topsoil and lastly the subsoil. When the hole is about 1.5 m deep, carefully clean a vertical face with a trowel and examine it.

What to look for in a soil profile

In a profile you can look at colour, life, texture and structure.

IN THE TOPSOIL	
Colour	*Indicates*
Dark brown or black	High in organic matter.
Greyish brown	Poor drainage, and acidity in a podsol horizon (see page 13).
Brown	Lots of soil life and nutrient cycling. Good drainage.

IN THE SUBSOIL	
Colour	*Indicates*
Grey	Waterlogged or very acid soil. Few nutrients.
Blue/green/grey and orange mottling	Seasonal waterlogging.
Uniform brown colour	Sufficient air. Good drainage.
Red	Related to parent material. If uniform, then well aerated.
Life	*Indicates*
Deep roots	Deep, friable soil.
Shallow roots	Compacted, waterlogged soil.
Lots of worms	Healthy soil.
Smell – sweet	Healthy soil.
– bad eggs	Waterlogged soil.

The parent rock

Let's get to the bottom of this. Parent rock breaks down slowly (weathers) and forms soil particles such as sand, silt, and clay. Some nutrients are also released for the plants and soil life. Most rocks are made of silica (SiO_2) plus variable amounts of aluminium, iron, calcium, sodium, potassium and magnesium. Some rocks are rich in certain foods, e.g. limestone has lots of calcium.

Description of profiles

The type of profile depends on the climate, vegetation, parent rock and age of the soil. Thousands of soil profile types have been recorded worldwide. Five profile types are shown below with comments on how to manage them. You may find something similar to one, or more, in your garden.

What does it all mean?

Name	Description	Origins	Cure/comment
Brown earth	Rich crumbly topsoil. Lighter subsoil (more compact but with little vertical cracks). General brown/yellow/red colour. Some clay in parent material. Deep roots. Lots of worms. Slightly acid.	Developed under warm, fairly dry conditions that favour growth of deciduous forest.	Excellent garden soil. ● If it contains a lot of silt, then do not overcultivate as this may impede water getting in.
Gley	Dark topsoil. Lighter subsoil with rusty (when dry) or blue/grey (when wet) mottling. Some clay in parent material. Shallow roots. Few worms. In severely waterlogged soils, smells of bad eggs.	Wet due to surface waterlogging or from a ground water table.	Potentially fertile but prone to waterlogging. ● Add organic matter to help hold air. ● Double dig to aerate. ● May need draining.
Podsol	Black surface. Pale brown to white beneath. Red/brown layer in subsoil often cemented into a pan. Few worms. Low in nutrients. Acidic.	Formed on heathland or under woodland over sand or sandstone. Rainfall washes iron and clay into subsoil.	A poor infertile soil. Easy to dig. Subsoil has an ashy appearance when top layers mixed. ● Add organic matter to retain nutrients. ● Mulch to prevent leaching. ● Add lime to raise pH. ● Break up pan.
Calcareous	Shallow dark topsoil, often neutral, with pure chalk or limestone beneath. Drains rapidly. Deeper soils have red/brown subsoil. Some soils contain clay.	Formed over limestone.	Alkaline, so many nutrients not available to plant. Good for plants liking calcareous soils. ● Add *no* lime. ● Increase depth of topsoil (with organic matter and green manures). This will help to prevent plants drying out, can make the soil less alkaline and feed the plants. ● Soils containing clay need organic matter to help cultivation.
Organic	Rich in humus. Dark brown/black colour. If over 50% organic matter which is over 45 cm thick, then classed as peat soils.	*Bog peat* Made of residues of sedges, heathers and mosses which decay slowly in wet soils to give acid peat.	Fairly infertile. May require drainage.
		Fen peat Made of residues of reeds, rushes and sedges. Forms at the edges of slow-moving water. These soils are usually less acid because the water coming to them may have previously moved over chalk and limestone.	An excellent soil, high in organic matter and available nitrogen. May need to add compost rich in phosphate and potash. Many plants will grow at a lower pH in an organic soil than in a mineral soil.

In general, topsoils can be improved by adding organic matter and using green manures. Subsoils are important for drainage. If porous and light, then organic matter can be added to retain water. If heavy clay, then drainage or double digging may help. Organic matter, lime (on acid soils) and gypsum (on neutral/alkaline soils) also help to break up clay.

What is soil made of?

The mineral particles – soil texture

The soil within the profile contains different sized mineral particles – sand, silt and clay. The feel of a soil depends to a great extent on the relative proportions of these different sized particles and is known as soil texture.

Texture is established during soil formation and will not change appreciably in our lifetime. The soil in your garden will remain 'a sandy soil' or 'a clay soil' whatever you do to it. Although the mineral particles in the soil are usually mixed up with organic matter, air, water and soil life, the basic sizes of the particles have a great influence on plant growth. Each type of soil has its advantages and disadvantages, and, by working out the texture, you can make the most of the advantages and minimise the disadvantages through good soil management.

Soil texture affects:
● the timing and type of soil cultivation
● the nutrient-holding capacity of the soil
● the drainage characteristics of the soil
● the amount of air and water that the soil can hold
● the soil temperature
● the structure of the soil
● the susceptibility of the soil to erosion
● the types of plants best suited to your garden

The sizes of the soil particles are divided into three classes, excluding gravel which is over 2 mm.

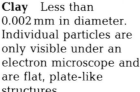

Sand Particles between 2 mm and 0.06 mm in diameter.
Visible to the naked eye. Usually made of quartz.

Silt Between 0.06 mm and 0.002 mm in diameter. Particles can only be seen under a microscope.

Clay Less than 0.002 mm in diameter. Individual particles are only visible under an electron microscope and are flat, plate-like structures.

Most soils contain a mixture of these particles and those with a fair mixture of sizes are called loams. These combine the characteristics listed above, so the gritty, silky and sticky feel are less obvious. A clay loam contains more clay, a medium loam has 50% sand and 50% silt and clay, and a sandy loam contains more sand. Many people refer to clay loams as heavy and sandy loams as light. This relates to the ease with which the soils can be worked and does not concern weight. A spadeful of light soil actually weighs more than the same volume of heavy soil!

How to work out your soil texture

The texture of a soil (sand/silt/clay) and type of soil (also including chalk and peat) can be worked out easily by feeling the soil. Take out about half a handful of topsoil and if dry, then add water gradually until the particles present form a ball. No excess water should be present. Knead the soil until it is moist throughout and remove any lumps.

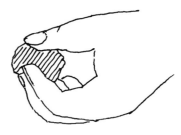

The flow chart and physical properties of the different soil particles are shown opposite and will help you assess the texture. It is important to note the contribution of additional materials, such as organic matter and calcium carbonate, because these can affect the feel of the soil. These can be assessed by looking at the soil or examining a profile.

How to work out your soil type

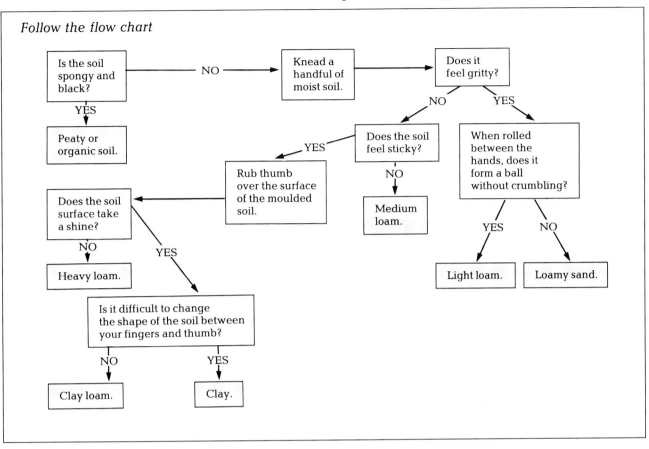

Follow the flow chart

Further tests and their interpretation

Work the moistened soil sample between your finger and thumb, held close to your ear. Note the sound and feel. Smear a 'ribbon' of the paste on the ball of the thumb; note the surface produced. If silt or heavier, then roll out a thin worm on the palm and see if it will form a circle without breaking. A little sand may be felt in soils which otherwise answer tests for silt or clay loam. These are sandy silt loams or sandy clay loams. The prefix 'stony' may be added when necessary.

Feel/sound	Plasticity		Result
Feels gritty, rasping sound when worked between finger and thumb held close to the ear.	Does not soil fingers after drying.		Sand
	Does soil fingers.	Will not readily mould into a cohesive ball.	Loamy sand
		Will easily form a cohesive ball.	Sandy loam
Feels soapy/silky. Squeaky sound!	'Ribbon' traversed by fine cracks. Soils fingers (silt adheres). Dry pellets crush to a silky dust.	Pudding fairly easily deformed. 'Worm' will not form a circle.	Silt loam
Feels sticky. Very little sound.	'Ribbon' smooth and shiny. Very smooth feel. Does not soil fingers (clay coheres – sticks to itself).	Moderate resistance to deforming. 'Worm' easily forms a circle.	Clay loam
	Dry pellets are not easily crushed between finger and thumb.	Resistance to deforming much greater.	Clay

Advantages and disadvantages of different soil types

Once you know what soil you have, you must then find out what it means. Probably, your soil will have characteristics of one or a combination of the following types. (For details on the management of these types, see pages 41–43.)

Calcareous
- Drain easily.
- Deep soils are quite fertile and support a wide range of crops.
- Shallow limestone soils suffer from drought.
- Alkaline, therefore some plant nutrients are limited (see page 33).

Silty
- If well structured, then can hold a lot of available water (see page 21).
- If cultivated when wet, then can pack down into a dense, cold, airless soil.
- Erode easily.

Peaty
- High in organic matter.
- Plants will tolerate a lower pH than in a mineral soil.
- Fen peats are fertile and productive.
- Fen peats are usually high in nitrogen but may need extra phosphate and potassium.
- Bog peats are acidic and infertile.
- Bog peats are deficient in copper and nitrogen.
- Often waterlogged.

Sandy
- Easy to work.
- Warm up quickly in the spring and can be cultivated earlier than other soil types.
- Suitable for early vegetable crops.
- Free draining.
- Nutrients easily washed out.
- Can become acid, particularly in areas of high rainfall.
- Can form a hard crust on the surface (cap) preventing emergence of delicate seedlings such as carrots.
- In dry weather plants can suffer from drought.

Clay

● May contain a rich supply of nutrients.

● Support a wide range of crops when managed well.

● Slow to warm in spring.

● Slow draining and, therefore, prone to water-logging.

● Sticky and difficult to work when wet.

● Shrink and form hard clods when dry which are practically impossible to break down until moistened again.

● Form deep, wide cracks in dry weather which break roots and lose moisture.

Clays – the secrets revealed

Clays have remarkable properties and if you get to understand how they work, then you can manage them to get an excellent fertile soil. Nature breaks rocks down into sand and silt, and finally into the minerals on which the rocks are based – silica and hydrated alumina. Clay-sized particles are usually crystalline structures, formed from these and other minerals.

How plants feed from clays

When plant roots breathe they produce positive charges (H+) in the soil called cations. They swop these for the foods on the clay. In fertile soils, the soil life breaks down bedrock and organic matter to replace the food on the plates again.

Sand does not have electrical charges and cannot hold onto plant foods.

Clays

● Are flat, plate-like structures.

● Have a negative electrical charge.

● Can hold onto some plant foods which have positive charges (especially calcium), like nails attaching to a magnet.

● Swell up when wet.

● Shrink when dry.

● Have colloidal properties (form a cloudy suspension in water).

● Have a large surface area. If all the clay plates in 28 g of clay were laid end to end and side by side, then they would cover an area of 6 acres – 24,000m^2.

Clays and lime

Clay plates are so small that they can wash into and clog up small soil pores, and also stick together to form a sticky mass, like wet sheets of paper. Lime and gypsum both contain calcium which has two positive charges and can attach to and link the plates together. This forms soil crumbs and improves soil structure. High rainfall can leach calcium carbonate out of the soil, making clays acid and sticky.

Clays and humus

These two have a very intimate relationship and bond together strongly to form stable little crumbs, with a great potential for holding on to plant food.

Clays and salt

When the sea floods the land and salt gets onto clays an unmanageable sticky mess can result. Salt contains sodium, with only one positive charge, so it cannot link clay plates together. Urine, an old-fashioned nitrogen feed, contains a lot of salt and its use on clay soil is not recommended. Salt can be removed from clay soils by applying gypsum.

Gypsum

Plants for your garden

Stop and think before you buy an array of seeds and plants or acquire armfuls of cuttings. Will the plants like growing in your soil? Sandy, silty or clay soils will support a wide range of plants with the correct management, but the plants listed below grow particularly well.

Soils over limestone and chalk, and peaty soils, are more particular. The former soils are alkaline and, therefore, many nutrients can become unavailable. Peaty soils, on the other hand, are usually acidic. Plants that are tolerant of these soils, without major pH adjustment, are listed.

Soil	Flowers	Shrubs	Vegetables	Fruit
Sandy	Yarrow *Achillea* spp Aubrietia *Aubrietia* spp Campion *Lychnis* spp Phlomis *Phlomis* spp Euphorbia *Euphorbia* spp Phygelius *Phygelius* spp Sedum *Sedum* spp Cranesbill *Geranium* spp	Artemesia *Artemesia* spp Broom *Cytisus* spp Rock rose *Helianthemum* spp Bramble *Rubus* spp Barberry *Berberis* spp Eleagnus *Eleagnus* spp Rose of Sharron *Hypericum* spp Cotoneaster *Cotoneaster* spp	Carrots Parsnips Asparagus Onion family Runner beans Tomatoes	Oranges Grapes Blackberries Nut trees
Silt/clay	Rose *Rosa* spp Marigold *Tagetes* spp Pearl everlasting *Anaphalis* spp Comfrey *Symphytum* spp Brunnera *Brunnera* spp Barrenwort *Epimedium* spp Hellebore *Helleborus* spp Hepatica *Hepatica* spp Ivy *Hedera* spp	Flowering currant *Ribes* spp Snowberry *Symphoricarpus* spp Spotted laurel *Aucuba* spp Skimmia *Skimmia* spp Mahonia *Mahonia* spp Hazel *Corylus* spp Aronia *Aronia* spp	Leeks Potatoes Broad beans Summer cabbages Courgettes Jerusalem artichokes Kale	Raspberries Plums Pears Red and white currants Blackcurrants Gooseberries
Chalky	Peony *Paeonia* spp Anemone *Anemone* spp Peruvian lily *Alstroemeria* spp Bleeding heart *Dicentra* spp Primula *Primula* spp Hosta *Hosta* spp Columbine *Aquilegia* spp Sweet pea *Lathyrus* spp Pink *Dianthus* spp Campion *Lychnis* spp	Mock orange *Philadelphus* spp Lilac *Syringa* spp Buddleia *Buddleia* spp Wintersweet *Chimonanthus* spp Periwinkle *Vinca* spp Spiraea *Spiraea* spp Yucca *Yucca filamentosa* Forsythia *Forsythia* spp Clematis *Clematis* spp	Beet Broccoli Cauliflowers Asparagus Spinach	Stone fruits Soft fruits (except strawberries and raspberries)
Peaty	Lily *Lilium* spp Lupin *Lupinus* spp Ornamental onion *Allium* spp Gentian *Gentiana* spp Woodrush *Luzula maxima* Nomocharis *Nomocharis* spp Masterwort *Astrantia* spp Loosestrife *Lythrum* spp Loosestrife *Lysimachia* spp Carex *Carex* spp Astilbe *Astilbe* spp	Broom *Cytisus* spp Gorse *Ulex* spp Rock rose *Helianthemum* spp Bearberry *Archostaphylos* spp Rhododendron *Rhododendron* spp Azalea *Rhododendron* spp Pieris *Pieris* spp Camellia *Camellia* spp Trumpet vine *Campsis radicans* Fothergillia *Fothergillia* spp Chilean bellflower *Lapageria* spp Lithospermum *Lithospermum* spp Nyssa *Nyssa* spp	Potatoes Onions Celery Roots Rhubarb	Blueberries Cranberries (on very acid soils) Apples and Strawberries (can tolerate pH 5.1) Raspberries
		Plants can survive at a lower pH in organic soils than in mineral soils.		
Salty (coastal)	Yarrow *Achillea* spp African lily *Agapanthus* spp Thrift *Armeria maritima* Cornflower *Centaurea* spp Sea holly *Eryngium* spp Statice *Limonium* spp Livingstone daisy *Mesembryanthemum* spp Stonecrop *Sedum* spp	Maple *Acer* spp Strawberry tree *Arbutus* spp Buddleia *Buddleia* spp Hebe *Hebe* spp Holly *Ilex* spp Cotton lavender *Santolina* spp Yucca *Yucca* spp	Asparagus Beet Cabbages Seakale Salad crops	Figs
		Coastal areas are often windy too, so a windbreak will help the plants grow.		

Other soil components – organic matter and humus

Organic matter in soils comes mainly from dead plant material and animal manures. It is a very complex substance and we do not fully understand what it is made of, but we do know that it has a remarkable range of functions. The plant remains contain organic compounds, sugars, starches, proteins, waxes and many more complicated molecules! In warm soils, with plenty of soil life and a good balance of air and water, the organic matter is broken down, the easy bits first, such as sugars, and the 'chewy' bits, such as woody materials, last. All the soil helpers, from the worms to the bacteria, take part in various stages of this grand feast. During the decay carbon dioxide is given off. Finally, an amazing substance called humus is formed, which is fairly resistant to further decay. Your garden soil may contain humus that is a few hours old next to ancient humus of over a thousand years old. Humus benefits the structure of the soil in many ways and has similar properties no matter where it was formed or from what organic materials. Humus is a formless, black, spongy, jelly-like substance containing a wide range of complex life chemicals. As with organic matter, it is what it does, not what it is, that counts. Humus has charges like clay and can hold on to nutrients. It also sticks to soil particles and helps

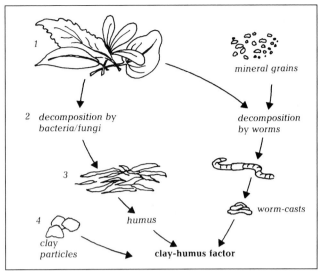

Humification of leaf litter and formation of clay-humus complexes

soil crumbs form, which make the soil friable and easier to work.

Humus is eventually broken down by the soil life, releasing food and gases. In your garden you are continuously removing organic matter and potential humus in the form of crops and prunings. The organic matter breaks down more rapidly in sandy soils and when soils are cultivated, as there is more air. In waterlogged soils peat is formed. Without air, the organic matter cannot break down, and peat bogs may be over 100 cm thick! (For further details on organic matter management, see pages 24 and 25.)

Decaying organic matter
- Is a home for soil life.
- Is a store cupboard of well-balanced food for soil life and, therefore, plant roots.
- Improves the structure of a wide range of soils.
- Holds both air and water.
- Stabilises mineral soils.
- Warms the soil, as the dark colour absorbs heat.
- Stimulates soil life.
- Mops up excess nutrients.
- Mops up potentially toxic elements like lead, some pesticides and copper.
- Has a high cation exchange capacity, like clays.
- Protects the soil from the weather and your cultivations.
- Buffers the soil against pH changes.
- Stimulates plant growth.
- Some parts break down quickly releasing food, while other parts remain in the soil for years.

To maintain organic matter levels in your soil
- Replace what you take off.
- Try to use materials that are going to be of immediate benefit, such as those that do not rob the soil of nitrogen:
  composted plant materials,
  composted strawy animal manures,
  leaf mould,
  green manures, dug in at the appropriate time.
- Encourage soil life to break down organic matter into humus by:
  keeping cultivation to a minimum,
  building up a good soil structure,
  aiming for a pH of about 6.5,
  making sure that the soil life have enough air and water to get on with the job,
  keeping the soil warm with mulches and cloches.
- Maintain your organic matter, once in place, by:
  covering the soil,
  keeping cultivation to a minimum.

Soil structure

The mineral particles and organic matter in the soil do not just form a simple mixture but are organised into aggregates or crumbs. This forms the soil structure. The structure of a soil is similar to the structure of a building. Buildings are held together by chalk and clay in cement, and, in some cases, organic matter where old cob walls or wattle and daub are found. Soil particles are held together by similar compounds. A building is designed by an architect, the soil by nature, but both work to the same goal to provide a good design for the benefit of the inhabitants. In a building, people work and live in the rooms; in the soil, the pores between the crumbs are where all the action takes place – drainage, aeration, passage of roots and residence of the soil organisms. Cultivation of soils would be virtually impossible without structure. Soil management aims to get or reclaim a good soil structure.

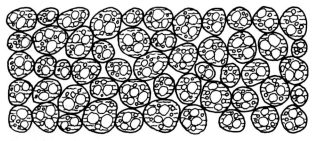

Aggregates

What structures the soil?

If you crush a dried clod of good garden soil in your hands, then it will form crumbs which do not break down readily. In coarse sandy soils the sand particles themselves form the crumbs, but in most soils crumbs are made of a mixture of sand, silt, clay and organic matter. Crumbs are held together by:

- the organic matter
- plant roots
- fungal threads
- bacterial 'gums'
- worms (producing gums and casts)
- calcium carbonate
- other compounds, such as iron
- clay

There are four main types of structure found in the soil; crumbs, plates, blocks and prisms/columns.

Types of structure

Crumbs   Few mm in diameter. Associated with a good medium loam.

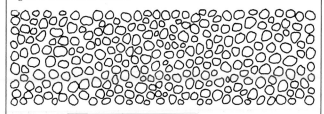

Blocks   Aggregates into irregular cube-like shapes, with spaces between for water to drain and roots to grow through. Found in soils which contain more clay and silt.

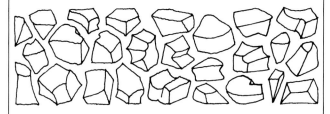

Columns/prisms   As clays shrink and swell the soil can crack, producing elongated structures between which roots can pass.

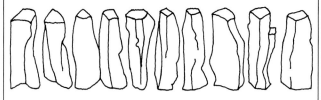

Plates   A horizontal structure with few vertical holes and cracks.

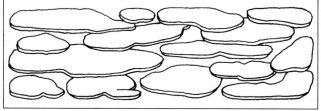

Soil structure changes with texture and depth. Crumbs are found in the top few centimetres of a soil covered in plants, ranging in size from a pin head to a pea. Deeper, the blocks become larger, ranging in size from sugar cubes to a spade. Like a building, the stability of the structure of a soil can vary. If a building is hit by a large force, then it will turn to rubble; so can soil. With soil there is a major difference: the strength depends on the water content. Soils go plastic when wet; buildings (hopefully) do not. Many soil structures are not water stable, and water can dissolve the gums and wash out the chemicals holding the crumbs together.

Pores in the soil – the living room

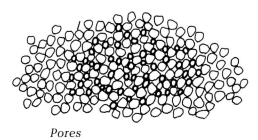

Pores

Soil contains living rooms: pores where the roots and soil organisms reside. A well-structured soil has:

● large pores, to allow air to get into the soil. Sand helps the formation of large pores

● small pores, to hold water. Silt, clay and organic matter help the formation of small pores

The pores form a network. Water can drain down through the large pores pulling in fresh air, and can be pulled up through the small pores (capillary action).

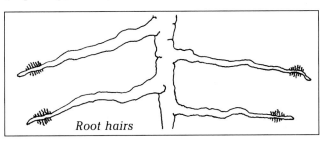

Root hairs

Roots grow through the network of large pores. Root hairs near their tips reach into the tiny water-filled pores to drink and feed. They are 1–2 mm long; if any shorter, then they would not be able to reach the water, if any longer, then they would drown from lack of air. Once again, nature has come up with the perfectly designed system.

Soil air

Soil air is needed by plant roots and soil life. It is found in any pores that do not contain water, but it contains more carbon dioxide than the air around us. It is vital to have porous soil to replenish the oxygen in the soil, just like good ventilation in a building. For adequate ventilation at least 10% of the soil needs to be filled with air.

Soil water

Plants need a lot of water:

● as part of their make-up

● as a transport system, to move nutrients around the plant

● for bodily functions, such as photosynthesis

● for rigidity

Over 98% of the water taken up by the root hairs is lost through the leaves by transpiration. It is essential, therefore, to make sure soils can keep up with the plants' demands. Some soil water is held in pores, while the excess drains away until it reaches the water table. The water content of the soil rises or falls depending on the quantity of rain or drought.

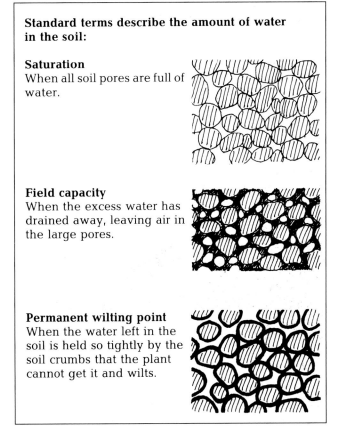

Standard terms describe the amount of water in the soil:

Saturation
When all soil pores are full of water.

Field capacity
When the excess water has drained away, leaving air in the large pores.

Permanent wilting point
When the water left in the soil is held so tightly by the soil crumbs that the plant cannot get it and wilts.

Available water
Between field capacity and wilting point the water is available to the plant roots. Sandy and most clay soils have relatively little available water. Sandy loams, silty loams and peaty soils hold most but need to be well structured to be of any use. Next time you are in the bath contemplating your garden, you can demonstrate water availability with a sponge. Dip it in the water, then hold it up. It is *saturated*. When all the excess water has dripped out it is at *field capacity*. Now squeeze it: all the water you can squeeze out is equivalent to *available water* and that left in the sponge represents the amount left in the soil at *permanent wilting point*.

Watering the soil
If a soil has dried out, then a sprinkling of water does very little; the soil has to be wetted to field

capacity before the next layer gets wet at all. At least 10.5 litres per sq m are needed to wet it. Sandy soils are very porous and water drains down quickly. When dry clay soils are watered, the water goes down cracks and is pulled up through the small pores from beneath.

Seedlings and transplants which have shallow roots need more frequent watering than established plants.

How to conserve water

● Add organic matter.

● Mulch a moist soil.

● Break up pans to allow roots to grow deeper in dry conditions and tap water. Breaking up pans also helps drainage if it is too wet.

How to achieve good structure

A good soil structure is usually found beneath a permanent meadow or under a wood where roots and soil life abound. The organic gardener can learn a lot from nature in order to create a good structure. Well-structured soils give deep rooting, active soil inhabitants, a good balance between air and water, and are stable and self reliant. Building up a good structure can take time, so be patient. Carefully managed, a well-structured soil can produce good plants for generations, so it is well worth the effort. It is a good idea to look for signs of good and bad structure when there is a drought or after very heavy prolonged rain. It is in these conditions that the plant growth will be most affected.

SIGNS OF GOOD STRUCTURE

Good plant growth.

Deep rooting.

Friable, crumbly soil (dry).

Friable, crumbly soil (wet).

Even brown colour.

Smell of sweet earth.

Lots of worms.

Network of visible pores and cracks in the soil profile.

Good drainage.

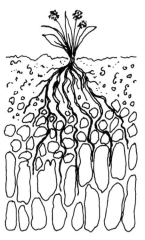

HOW TO ACHIEVE GOOD STRUCTURE

Add organic matter to help crumb structure, hold water and air.

Add lime (if acid), gypsum (if alkaline) to clays.

Encourage soil life.

Break up any platey structures.

Drain if necessary.

Subsequent cultivations

Keep to a minimum.

Keep as shallow as possible.

Cultivate when soil is *just* moist.

Let the worms and roots dig the soil.

Protection

Keep covered with mulches, green manures or crop.

Minimum exposure of bare soil to rain.

Try not to walk on the soil.

Use a bed system.

SIGNS OF BAD STRUCTURE

Poor plant growth.

Shallow rooting, confined to a few cracks or earthworm channels.

Soil in hard lumps or like dust (dry).

Sticky, airless mass (wet).

Patches of grey/red soil.

Few worms (this could also mean an acid soil).

Soil layer or pan in boundary between topsoil and subsoil.

Moss on surface when wet.

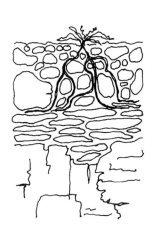

HOW BAD STRUCTURE ARISES

Compaction – through walking on soil.

Compaction of subsoil – through rotovating (possible on clay, silty and sandy soils).

Heavy irrigation/rain – washes gums away; physically breaks up crumbs.

Lack of organic matter.

Digging when wet and plastic.

Overcultivation, e.g. raking dry soil excessively.

Having a bare soil.

Overcropping the garden.

On clay soils that contain salt.

SOIL MANAGEMENT

Managing your soil

Now that you know something about your soil, you can look after it and provide the ideal conditions for the plant roots and soil life. The most important aspect of soil management is getting a good soil structure. This will encourage the soil life to thrive, feed plants and help them to grow an extensive root system and obtain essential food, water and air. Organic matter is absolutely necessary in soil management because it helps to structure all types of soils and also provides, among other things, food for soil life.

It is possible to improve your garden soil by changing the texture – adding sand to heavy soil and clay to sandy soil, called marling. This was once common practice but is not very practical in a garden. For example, a plot of sandy loam about 8 m by 3 m contains about 10,200 kg of topsoil. You would have to add over 1,000 kg of clay to make any appreciable difference in the texture.

In the following pages, therefore, I will concentrate on ways of managing soils by improving and maintaining good structure. Different types of soils require different management techniques to achieve the same result and these are dealt with on pages 41 to 43.

What does soil management involve?

Management	Result
Addition of organic matter.	Improves and maintains the structure of a wide range of soils. Aids drainage in clays and silty soils, and improves water-holding capacity of sandy soils. Provides all the needs for healthy soil organisms and plant roots. Feeds the soil.
Creating a well-drained soil with sufficient water reserves.	Prevents structure breaking down. Encourages healthy soil and deep-rooting plants.
Cultivating the soil, in the right state at the right time.	Breaks up bad structures, such as pans, thus improving drainage. Creates a suitable seedbed for seeds and seedlings.
Creating a no-dig system (in conjunction with keeping the soil covered and avoiding compaction by walking on it).	Enables soil life to function and provides a good structure, imitating the way nature cares for the soil.
Using green manures whenever and wherever possible.	Digs, feeds, structures and protects the soil. Protects soil structure.
Covering the soil with a mulch.	Protects soil structure. Some mulches feed the soil.
Rotation of crops.	Increases plant health and vigour. Reduces the need for cultivation. Enables the soil to replenish lost nutrients. Makes the best use of your resources, such as compost and manure.
Checking and, if necessary, adjusting soil pH.	Encourages a healthy soil population. Ensures nutrients in the soil are available to plants. Reduces pests and diseases.
Lime/gypsum.	Feeds and structures soil.
Fertilisers/nutrients.	Feed the soil.

Organic matter

Organic matter and 'humified', or rotting, organic matter can improve the structure of a wide range of soils. It comes in many forms and can be used in a variety of ways.

Compost
Every gardener should make compost.
- Improves soil structure and feeds the soil life.
- Kills weed seeds and some diseases, and recycles garden and kitchen waste.
- Approximate nutrient content: 0.5% nitrogen (N), 0.25% phosphate (P_2O_5), 0.8% potash (K_2O). Full range of trace elements.

Composted animal manures
These are a useful import to the garden.
- Composted strawy manures, from horses and cattle, improve soil structure and feed soil life.
- Chicken and pigeon manures are very strong and are best used as an activator in compost.
- Avoid manures from intensive farms which can be contaminated.
- Composted strawy manures are available commercially in bags.
- Approximate nutrient content of farmyard manure: 0.6% N, 0.25% P_2O_5, 0.4% K_2O. Full range of trace elements.

Leaf mould
- Leaves from gardens or parks can be returned to the soil after decaying.
- Leaf mould improves soil structure but contains less nutrients.
- Leaves take two to three years to decay in wire containers or ventilated bin liners.

Mushroom compost
- An excellent soil conditioner and food for soil life.
- The product is alkaline and should not be used on acid-loving plants.
- Mushroom compost from non-organic sources may contain pesticide residues.
- Approximate nutrient content: 0.7% N, 0.3% P_2O_5, 0.3% K_2O. Full range of trace elements.

Fine Bark   Compost   Animal manure   Mushroom compost

Leaf mould   Spent hops   Cocoa shell   Coir dust

Cocoa shell

● Cocoa bean shells from the chocolate industry.

● Dig in or use as a mulch to improve structure.

● Holds water and may repel slugs.

● Use on mature plants as it contains salts which may damage seedlings.

● Approximate nutrient content: 2.8% N, 0.4% P_2O_5, 3.2% K_2O. Full range of trace elements.

● Apply at a quarter of the rate of other composts. The product is awaiting inspection from the Soil Association, who give products an official stamp of approval.

Spent hops

● A by-product of the brewing industry.

● Can be used as a mulch or to dig in.

● Improves soil structure and provides food for soil life.

● Approximate nutrient content: 0.5% N, 1.5% P_2O_5, 0.5% K_2O. Full range of trace elements.

Straw, bark products and sawdust

● Contain a lot of carbon and can add to the organic matter content of the soil.

● Use as a mulch to protect soil structure around well-established plants.

● Compost before use to allow any toxic compounds to decompose.

● Tree products contain few nutrients.

Coir dust

● A peat alternative and a by-product of the coconut industry.

● Improves soil structure, holds more water and lasts longer than peat.

● pH 5.5 to 6.3.

● Contains few nutrients.

● Generally used in potting compost because it is expensive to use as a soil conditioner. However, peat is also 'environmentally' expensive.

Seaweed

● Does not contribute to the bulk of the soil.

● Improves soil structure because it contains gums which bind soil particles together.

● Approximate nutrient content: 0.3% N, 0.1% P_2O_5, 1.0% K_2O. Full range of trace elements.

For further details refer to the companion handbook in this series, *How to make your Garden Fertile* by Pauline Pears.

HOW TO APPLY

Unrotted woody materials

● e.g. straw, bark, shredded stemmy plant material.

● Use as a mulch on moist/warm soils around established plants.

● Do not dig into the soil as the bacteria may rob the soil of nitrogen, causing plants to go yellow.

● Avoid weeds and diseased materials.

Rotted materials

● e.g. compost, composted animal manures, leaf mould and mushroom compost.

● Can be dug into the surface because the bacteria have already sorted out their nitrogen requirements in the composting process.

● Avoid putting the material below the reach of soil organisms (20 cm) because this can restrict root growth and does not improve the structure of the topsoil.

● Avoid *fresh* manure in contact with plant roots.

● Can also be used as a surface mulch around perennials, transplanted annuals or as a thin layer on a seedbed.

HOW MUCH AND WHEN

● The amount applied is as long as a piece of string. A rough guide is a barrowload of composted materials to 3–4 sq m. It depends partly on the soil texture; a barrowload will have a greater effect on a sandy than a clay soil. If too much is applied, then plants may put on unwanted lush growth or the nutrients may be washed out of the soil. Leaf mould and composts with few plant nutrients can be used in larger quantities.

● To avoid waste, apply as, or just before, plants are growing, e.g. in spring or before sowing a green manure in autumn.

● Apply to the soil when it is moist and warm.

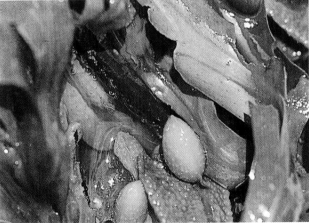

Seaweed

Green manures

Green manures are plants that are grown and put straight back into the soil.

What do green manures do?
- Cover the soil to protect the structure.
- Prevent plant foods from washing out.
- Suppress weeds.
- Encourage worms and other soil life.
- Reduce erosion.
- Dig the soil.
- Improve drainage.
- Bring up nutrients from the subsoil.
- Fertilise the soil, especially green manures from plants that fix nitrogen.
- Add to the organic matter in the soil.
- Increase the health of the soil.

Incorporating green manures
Green manures are usually returned to the soil a few weeks before planting a crop.
- The ideal stage to turn them in is just before they get tough and woody.
- If dug in when soft and sappy, then they will supply nutrients but little organic matter.
- If left until woody, then they are difficult to incorporate and may cause nitrogen robbery.
- Tough green manures can be used as a mulch or added to compost.
- Do not let them seed and become weeds.
- Mow or cut the green manure and allow to wilt, then either dig in the chopped up material or mulch and let the worms take it down.
- Some green manures, e.g. mustard, die after frost and gradually decompose. Plant your crop once the green manure has decomposed. Decomposition can take from a few days to a few weeks, depending on the season, type of green manure and stage of growth.
- Green manures can be used in many ways. A few examples are shown opposite.

For further information refer to the companion volume in this series, *How to make your Garden Fertile* by Pauline Pears.

Winter grazing rye *Secale cereale*
Sow at 30g/sq m up to mid October. Good overwintering crop. Sometimes difficult to turn in. Adds nitrogen if dug in when sappy; adds organic matter if dug in just before maturing.

Mustard *Sinapis alba*
Sow at 5g/sq m from March to the end of August. Fast-growing summer gap filler. Suppresses weeds but not winter hardy. Dig in *before* flowering. Shallow roots.

White clover *Trifolium repens*
Sow at 3g/sq m from April to July. Fixes nitrogen. Overwinters. Can be sown under widely spaced crops.

Winter tares *Vicia sativa*
Sow at 8g/sq m from April to the end of August or in late summer to overwinter. Produces large amounts of green matter, fixes nitrogen and has an extensive root system.

Mulches

A mulch is a covering of the soil surface and should be applied to a warm, moist soil to keep it so.

What do mulches do?
- Protect soil structure from rain.
- Suppress weeds.
- Keep soil moist and warm.
- Help to warm soil, if dark.
- Help to cool soil, if light.

Which mulch for which job?

Compost, grass mowings and straw
- Protect soil structure and feed the soil.
- If too thick, then the mowings will get hot and slimy, so use any excess mowings as an activator in the compost heap.
- Compost and composted manures make excellent mulches too; they feed the soil and improve structure as they are taken down by the soil life.

Straw under roses

Bark mulches and wood chippings
- Protect soil structure and look attractive.
- Use under established shrubs and perennials.

Wood chippings under young tree

- If you are concerned about the wood causing nitrogen robbery, then spread over newspaper or woven fleece to prevent incorporation.

Black polythene
- Suppresses weeds.
- Plant fruit and vegetables through it.
- Warms soil and brings on an early crop.
- White plastic mulches are also available. These give late crops because they cool the soil. Some gardeners use white mulches to hasten ripening in tomatoes.

Biodegradable paper
- A thick brown paper used on beds.
- Chop in to rot after use.
- Can shrink, so water and let it dry before planting crops through it.

More details on mulches are given in the companion volume in this series, *Weeds: How to control and love them* by Jo Readman.

Cultivation

Traditionally, forking and digging are used to cultivate the soil. Some gardeners use a no-dig system and leave nature to do the work; plant roots and soil organisms replace the spade. Both systems have their advantages and disadvantages.

Why cultivate the soil?

	Soil structure	Soil composition
Soil conditions present in autumn	Soil compacted by rain and trampling. Few soil pores and, therefore, possible waterlogging.	Nutrients removed by crops or washed out (leached) beyond reach of roots.
Soil conditions ideal for plant growth	Loose crumbs of soil to allow root growth and active soil life. Spaces in soil; small for water, large for air and drainage.	Nutrients in reach of young roots and available in soil water.
Effect of digging	Breaks soil into large clods (broken down by frost in winter). Loosens soil, forms spaces and improves drainage.	Buries weeds which decompose slowly to form a store of nutrients. Leached nutrients brought to surface.
The no-dig system	Soil never walked on and protected from rain by a mulch, crop or green manure. Cultivated by plant roots and soil life.	Nutrients retained in topsoil by surface mulching with organic matter. Green manures recycle nutrients in the topsoil. Cover prevents leaching by rain.

Advantages and disadvantages of digging

Advantages

- Breaks up subsurface pans.
- Kills annual weeds and surface-rooting perennials.
- Soil pests can be removed by hand or by predators.
- When left rough over winter, clays are broken down and many weeds and pests are killed by the frost.
- Appropriate for clearing and improving new ground.
- Good for preparation of an orchard because fruit cannot grow well on shallow or compacted soils.

Disadvantages

- Hard work!
- Can only be done in suitable conditions.
- Disturbs soil organisms.
- Soil may be left bare causing leaching of plant foods, capping by heavy rain and the blocking of pores by fine particles.

Digging

When to dig

- Clay soils are dug in autumn, to allow frost and the weather to break up the clay.
- Light soils can be dug in spring.
- Never dig frozen soil or one which is wet enough to stick to your wellies.

How to dig – basic rules

- Use a sharp, clean spade.
- Dig spadefuls that are easy to handle.
- Do not rush the job: stop when you feel tired. Many ardent diggers have damaged their backs by overdoing it!

Single digging

Work the soil to the depth of a spade or fork. This is adequate for soils which do not have a compacted subsoil. The trenches taken out should be about 30 cm wide.

Double digging

● Cultivates the soil to twice the depth of a spade.

● Useful for breaking new ground or subsoil pans.

● Improves the structure of the subsoil without bringing it to the surface.

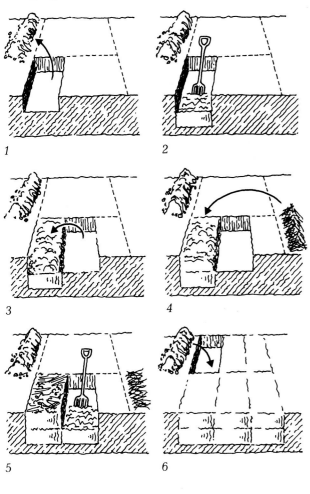

1. Divide the piece of land in half. Take out a trench 60 cm wide and one-spade's depth in one corner. Place the soil alongside the position of the final trench.
2. Loosen the base of the first trench with a fork.
3. Take out the next 60 cm wide trench and throw forward onto the first trench. Do not do this all at once, but work back several centimetres at a time.
4. Fork compost into the loosened topsoil.
5. Fork the bottom of the second trench. Continue working backwards across the plot, and avoid standing on the plot that you have dug. Finally, turn round and work back to the other end in the same way.
6. Fill in the last trench with the soil from the first, without having to carry it anywhere! In winter leave the soil in fist-sized clods or cover with a green manure.

No-dig systems

You can grow plants in a well-structured soil without digging at all. It is easy to see how permanent crops of perennial flowers, fruit and shrubs can be grown in this way. A mulch laid on moist soil after planting will protect the structure and the plant roots will do the rest.

Vegetables and annuals are a different matter, requiring tending and harvesting. The key is to be able to reach the plants without walking on the soil.

Keep off the soil

Grow plants in narrow fixed beds separated by permanent paths. A bed should be twice as wide as the length of your arm, about 120 cm, to allow all work to be carried out from the paths. Raised beds are recommended if drainage is poor or the soil shallow. To do this, put the topsoil from the paths onto them and add organic matter to the surface. If the soil is compacted, then double digging may be required before making the bed.

Advantages and disadvantages of fixed beds and no-dig systems

Advantages

● Avoids back-breaking digging and bending.

● Subsoil will stay where it belongs.

● Fertile topsoil will not get buried.

● Good structure will not be broken up by digging.

● Worms love them!

● No feet, no compaction.

● Crops can be harvested in any weather.

● No space is wasted.

● Soil surface is protected from rain by plants.

● No room for weeds if crops are spaced closely.

● Helps drainage of heavy soils.

● Far less time-consuming once set up.

● Many crops, such as carrots, can be pulled up. Brassicas should be dug out to avoid leaving any root pests in the soil.

Disadvantages

● Raised beds can dry out easily on light soils.

● Unfortunately, slugs, wireworms and other soil pests prefer no-dig systems.

● Mice like no-dig beds!

● Potatoes have a lower yield on bed systems.

Fixed beds and no-dig systems

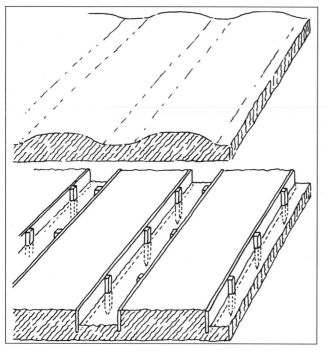

No-dig beds

Raised beds can:

● be convex or supported by boards

● be as long as practicable

● lie north to south, to take maximum advantage of the sun

● have paths wide enough for walking or a wheelbarrow

● slope 5°–10° towards the south to raise the temperature

Full cover

To keep off rain and maintain good structure:

● plant most crops close together

● Intercrop widely spaced plants, such as Brussels sprouts, with fast-growing crops like lettuce

● undersow widely spaced crops, such as sweetcorn, with green manures, such as alfalfa

● avoid leaving ground bare by using transplants rather than seeds

● grow green manures when there are no crops in the soil

● use a mulch to cover bare soil, and, to help decay, cut green manures before planting crops

The above points make better use of space, and close planting will help keep out weeds. The roots of green manures also help to loosen any compaction.

Mound cultivation

A novel system well worth trying is the mound. This is a cross between a deep bed and a compost heap.

● Lift turf off to 10 cm to give an area about 1.5 m wide and as long as practicable.

● Place woody material and branches to a depth and width of about 20 cm in the centre of the bed.

● Replace the turves (grass side down) like a clamp over the woody material.

● Add layers of well-rotted leaves, manure, coarse and fine compost.

In this system the layers gradually break down, slowly releasing food and providing humus-rich soil for four to five years. This system is ideal for hungry crops, such as courgettes, and also makes an excellent strawberry bed.

Mound cultivation

The chicken tractor

Chickens have many useful functions apart from laying eggs. A chicken tractor system uses chickens to clear ground of pests and weeds before planting. Many gardeners use their chickens to help turn in green manures and fertilise

plots with their manure before planting. Personally, I have more success doing it the other way around. The chickens are put on the soil in an ark after cropping. They scratch up and eat crop residues, soil pests and weeds, and turn it all into plant food. However, they compact the soil as they scratch and have dust baths. This can be remedied by sowing a green manure which also takes up any excess nitrogen from the strong manure.

The mechanical cultivator

Many gardeners are tempted by mechanical cultivators, but on a small plot they are not really necessary. They are more useful in preparing a seedbed than for digging because they create a fine tilth, and can also be used as a large hoe. Although they cultivate the surface, the weight of the machine can cause compaction further down and regular use may damage the soil structure.

Seedbed preparation

Many plants can be brought on from seed in an outdoor seedbed.

● Choose a site with plenty of sun but sheltered from wind.

● Dig the bed in autumn if it contains a lot of clay and/or if drainage is a problem.

● Over winter there are several options:
 – mulch with organic matter low in nitrogen, such as leaf mould, to protect the soil surface,
 – sow a green manure,
 – add lime or gypsum to heavy clays, and sow a deep-rooting green manure,
 – as a last resort, leave dug clay soil bare to allow weather action to break it up.

● Fork over the soil on a dry warm day in the spring (if green manures are present, then treat as shown on page 26).

● Cover soil with clear plastic or glass and leave for two weeks to:
 – encourage germination of weeds which can then be hoed off,
 – bring slugs to the surface, pick off,
 – protect the fine structure from rain damage,
 – warm the soil.

● On the next fine day, remove the cover and rake to a fine tilth. Some gardeners apply bone meal at 130 g/sq m to aid seed germination.

● Sow the seeds in drills or by broadcasting; water the base of the drills if the soil is dry.

● Cover seeds with dry or moist soil. On heavy soils, seeds such as carrots can be covered with a thin layer of fine compost to help germination.

● Water with a fine rose or a fine sprinkler to avoid damage to seedbed tilth.

Capping

Seedbeds are prone to capping; the structure of the soil surface breaks down to form a solid thin crust. Heavy rain is the main culprit and sandy and silty soils the main victims. To prevent capping:

● cover the surface with a non-woven polypropylene fleece

● put cloches over the plants but do not forget to water them

● add a thin layer of fine organic matter

If capping occurs, then hoe carefully between the rows to break it up. Water with a fine rose until seedlings emerge.

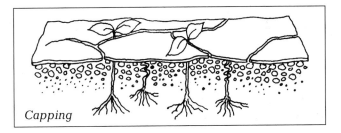
Capping

Puffy beds – or underconsolidation

In some seedbeds the soil may be too loose for the roots to contact soil particles and films of water. This occurs after frosty weather, especially on sandy and peaty soils. If the soil feels very light and fluffy and, dare I say, it sinks over 2.5 cm when you tread on it, then it may need consolidating. Do this by tamping down the soil gently with the back of a rake.

Transplants

When transplanting seedlings, make sure that the soil is not too wet and plastic as your trowel or dibber will have the same effect as a big boot! Many planters are available now that take a core or plug out of the soil which can then be replaced with your transplant.

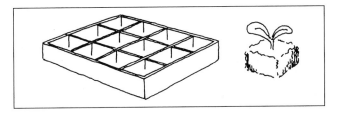

Crop rotation

Vegetables can be grouped into families which share similar nutrient requirements and have the same pest and disease problems. Crop rotation means that the family groups are not grown on the same piece of land every year. As well as preventing the build-up of soil-living pests and diseases, crop rotation makes soil management easier:

● deep-rooting and shallow-rooting crops can be alternated to tap the soil at different depths

● crops which do not cover the soil totally can be alternated with ones which do (e.g. potatoes) to protect soil structure

● hungry crops, such as brassicas, can follow crops which feed the soil (e.g. legumes) to balance nutrient requirements

● valuable organic matter can be added to crops that need it most to make the best use of resources

● lime and manure can be added in different years to prevent lime reacting with manure and releasing nitrogen to the air

● rotations can be planned to ensure the efficient use of green manures

An example of a four year rotation is given in the photograph above.

Crops which do not belong to these families, such as courgettes, sweetcorn and lettuce, can be given a separate year or fitted in where appropriate. However, they should still be moved around in rotation. These crops benefit from the addition of garden compost.

The rotation shown here is just an example, but there are many permutations. You can design a rotation that suits your personal needs and those of the plants and soil.

A four year rotation

Year	Crop	Additions to the soil	Other information
1	Potatoes/tomatoes, possibly followed by a green manure, e.g. rye.	Manure/compost.	Cover soil, protecting structure.
2	Peas/beans, possibly followed by a green manure.	None. Peas and beans fix their own nitrogen.	Benefit from the humus left by the potatoes. Covers the soil over winter.
3	Brassicas.	Lime, e.g. ground dolomitic limestone, or calcified seaweed.	Can be undersown with a leguminous green manure to protect soil.
4	Roots/onions, followed by a quick-growing green manure, such as mustard, before returning to potatoes.		Deep rooting.

Acidity and Alkalinity

Soil pH is a measure of acidity or alkalinity and is measured on a scale from 1 to 14. Soil pH ranges from about 3.5 to 8.5 and affects soil life, the structure, the nutrient availability and plant growth. Most plants prefer a soil pH of 6.3 to 6.8. Certain plants like soil that is slightly more acid or more alkaline but plants will not thrive below pH 4 and above pH 8.

pH of soil	LOW pH				Neutral		HIGH pH	
	<-------------------- Acid			--------------------------		--------------------------	Alkaline ---------->	
	3	4	5	6	7		8	9
Crop	Most crops fail	Conifers Heathers Rhododendrons Camellias Azaleas	Fine lawn grasses	Top and soft fruits thrive	Most crops	Brassicas Legumes	Spinach Clematis	Most crops fail

Harmful effects of acid soil

● Bacteria become less active.

● Rhizobia do not nodulate legumes below pH 5.7.

● Earthworms are generally absent below pH 4.5.

● Toxic substances can be released into the soil.

● Brassicas can get club root more easily.

● Plant growth is reduced.

Harmful effects of alkaline soil

● Lime can react with manure, releasing ammonia gas which wastes nitrogen fertiliser.

● Nutrients can become unavailable.

● Potatoes become prone to scab, a fungal disease.

AVAILABILITY OF NUTRIENTS

low acid   neutral — alkaline high
pH   4   5·   6   7   8 pH

nitrogen

phosphorus

potassium

calcium

magnesium

iron

manganese

Measuring soil pH

pH testing kits are available from most garden centres and come in a wide array of shapes and sizes. Full instructions for use are given with the kits.

Using the results

It is easier to grow ornamental plants that thrive in the soil you have, rather than try to change the pH level. (Suitable plants are listed on page 18 and above.) Azalea lovers: do not despair. It is possible to grow acid-loving plants in neutral soils by plunging them in pots filled with three parts acidic compost to one part sharp sand.

Most vegetables prefer a pH of about 6.5. Different plots within the rotation can benefit from pH adjustments. Potatoes thrive in acid soils (pH 5.5 to 6.0) where the disease scab cannot survive, while brassicas can be grown in soils of pH 6.5 to 7.0 to reduce the likelihood of club root. Both top and soft fruit like an acid soil (about pH 6.0).

Raising soil pH – making it more alkaline

● Add lime (see page 34).

● Comfrey liquid is alkaline and will raise soil pH slightly.

● Add mushroom compost (this contains a lot of chalk).

Lowering soil pH – making it more acidic

● Add composted manure, acid compost, cocopeat (about one barrowload per sq m).

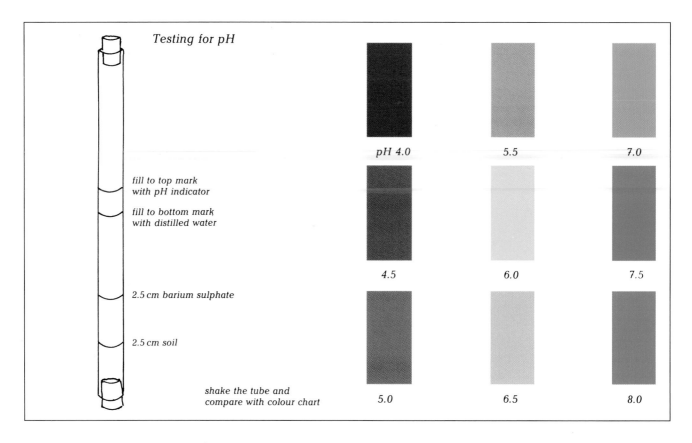

Testing for pH

fill to top mark
with pH indicator

fill to bottom mark
with distilled water

2.5 cm barium sulphate

2.5 cm soil

shake the tube and
compare with colour chart

pH 4.0   5.5   7.0

4.5   6.0   7.5

5.0   6.5   8.0

● Use raised beds on alkaline soils and mulch with acidic composts and manures. Raised beds also prevent runoff of lime-rich water from the surrounding land.

● Use walled raised beds filled with three parts acidic compost to one part sand to grow acid-loving plants, such as rhododendrons.

A general idea of soil pH can be gained from the plants growing, or should I say thriving, in your garden (see page 10). Hydrangeas act as a pH indicator. On alkaline soils the flowers are pink or red/purple, while on acid soils they turn blue or blue/purple!

Lime

Lime is a word loosely applied to materials containing calcium. These include limestone, chalk, slaked lime and ground dolomitic limestone.

Application of lime

● Apply to surface or gently fork into topsoil.

● Never apply with fresh manure or organic matter. Either dig in manure and apply lime to surface or leave a gap of about six months between manure and lime applications.

● Check soil pH annually to see if more lime is required; naturally occurring liming materials last for several years, and clay soils may require more liming than sandy soils.

● High rainfall washes out lime, so mulch soils in susceptible areas.

To lime or not to lime

● If your soil is pH 6.5 or above, then you will not need to lime. Overliming is damaging and can lock up plant nutrients.

● If lime and fresh manure are added together, then the nitrogen in the manure will be lost to the air in the form of ammonia.

What does lime do?

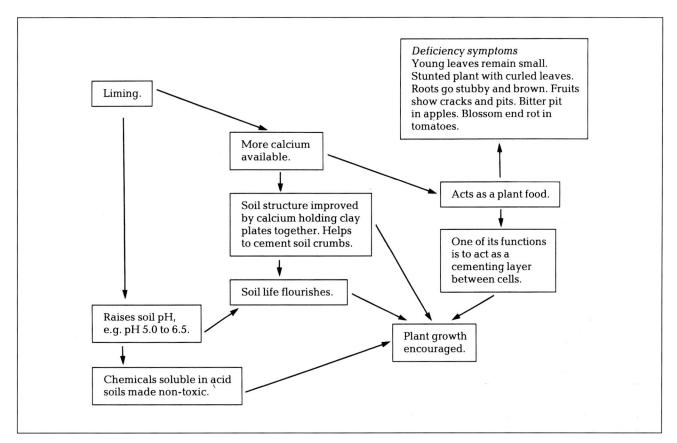

Lime application

Type of lime	Contains	When to apply	Quantity	Comment
Ground limestone, chalk	A natural rock containing calcium carbonate.	Autumn, annually until soil reaches desired pH.	250 g/sq m.	Neutralises acid soil. Slow release, gentle action. Supplies calcium.
Dolomite lime (maglime)	A natural rock containing calcium and magnesium carbonate.	Autumn, annually until soil reaches desired pH.	250 g/sq m.	Neutralises acid soil. Slow release, gentle action. Supplies calcium and magnesium.
Calcified seaweed	A coral made mainly of calcium carbonate.	Any time of year, to lawns and beds.	40 g/sq m.	Excellent soil conditioner. Neutralises acid soil. Slow release, gentle action. Supplies calcium, magnesium and trace elements. Do not use on soils over pH 6.5.
Marl	A mixture of clay and calcium carbonate.	Autumn, on clay soils.	As specified.	Useful on acid sandy soils as it contains clay and calcium. Neutralises acid soil.
Slaked lime, caustic lime, hydrated lime	Lime burnt and water added.	Do not apply.		Very soluble, very strong. Not recommended for use in the organic garden.
Gypsum	Calcium sulphate.	Autumn on beds, spring on lawns. Spike and brush in.	250 g/sq m then subsequently 40 g/sq m.	Does not affect soil pH. Corrects shortage of calcium and sulphur. Helps to break up clays on neutral and alkaline soils.

Plant nutrients

Plants get carbon (C), hydrogen (H) and oxygen (O) from air and water in photosynthesis. Other nutrients come from the soil. Nitrogen (N), phosphorus (P), potassium (K), magnesium (Mg) and calcium (Ca) are needed in fairly large quantities. Trace elements are needed in much smaller quantities but are still vital to plant growth. These include iron, zinc, copper, manganese, boron and molybdenum.

Chemical fertilisers are soluble in water and feed the plant directly. This is quick but has disadvantages.

● Plants can take up too much fertiliser, such as nitrogen, leading to sappy growth. Such plants are more prone to pests and diseases.

● Plants can take up too much of one nutrient and not enough of another, e.g. plants fed with too much potassium get magnesium deficiency and turn yellow.

● Plants may not get the right balance of trace elements. Molybdenum only accounts for 0.00001% of the plant's nutrients but if not available, then plants will be deformed and stunted.

Organic gardeners rely on recycled bulky materials, such as composts and green manures, to feed the soil life which then releases soluble food to the plants in a slow, balanced way.

Occasionally, a supplement or 'pick-me-up' tonic is required and this is where organic fertilisers fit in. These are fertilisers of organic origin that are not very soluble, and they feed the soil life but do not add to the organic matter of the soil. Supplements are used when:

● high demands are made of your soil, e.g. growing several crops a year

● one nutrient is needed to cure a deficiency

● organic materials are not available

● the garden is getting started

● plants need a 'tonic', e.g. after being ravaged by a pest

To get the most out of bulky organic materials and fertilisers you need:

● a good soil structure

● a warm soil; the soil life works best above 6°C

● the right pH. A soil which is too acid or alkaline can upset the soil life and make nutrients unavailable

● organic matter/humus or clay to hold onto soil nutrients and prevent them washing out

For further details on nutrients and deficiencies refer to the companion volume in this series, *Healthy Fruit & Vegetables: How to avoid diseases, disorders and deficiencies* by Pauline Pears and Bob Sherman.

Which nutrient for which job?

Nutrient	What it does	Deficiency	Where it comes from
Nitrogen (ammonia or nitrate)	Makes protein. Makes plants green. Helps leaves and shoots to grow.	Older leaves turn yellow. Plants are stunted. Nitrates can easily wash out of the soil.	Well-rotted organic matter: nitrogen does not come from rock. Legumes, green manures. Blood, fish and bone meal. Hoof and horn. Seaweed meal. Hair, nettles, feathers, nitrifying bacteria (azotobacter).
Phosphorus (phosphate)	Important in root growth, germination and seedling development.	Stunted roots. Blue/green hue on old leaves. Does not wash out easily but becomes unavailable at low and high pHs.	Organic matter. Rock phosphate (apatite). Blood, fish and bone meal. Bone meal. The fungus mycorrhiza can help plants to take up phosphate.
Potassium (potash)	Makes protein. Affects the size and quality of fruits and flowers. Increases frost, pest and disease resistance. Influences the uptake of other nutrients.	Stunted plants. Yellow/brown edge to leaves. Potash washes out easily but can attach to clay and organic matter.	Organic matter. Rock potash. Seaweed. Comfrey. Wood ash from young twigs can easily be washed out of the soil.

Magnesium	Makes the green pigment chlorophyll.	Yellowing between leaf veins. Affects older leaves first.	Organic matter. Dolomitic limestone. Seaweed.
Calcium	Makes protein. Cements cells together.	Classic symptoms include: blossom end rot in tomatoes, tip burn in lettuce. Washed out by rain.	Organic matter. Mushroom compost. Limes. Gypsum. Certain weeds, such as chamomile, comfrey, silverweed, horsetail. A healthy soil helps plants take up calcium.
Sulphur	Makes protein and chlorophyll. Needed by brassicas and onions.	Stunting, yellowing. Rare.	Organic matter. Seaweed. Gypsum.
Trace elements	Wide range of functions.	Wide range of symptoms.	Organic matter. Healthy fertile soil. Seaweed meal. Liquid seaweed and liquid animal manures. Mycorrhiza (see page 5).

Organic fertilisers and minerals – the supplements

Analyses are approximate and vary according to source.
Nutrients expressed as nitrogen (N), phosphate (P_2O_5), and potash (K_2O).

Fertiliser	Nutrient (%)	Use	Application	Comment
Blood, fish and bone	N: 3.5 P_2O_5: 8.0 K_2O: 0.0 Trace: 0.0	A general fertiliser for leaf and root growth.	200 g/sq m. Use as base dressing (before planting) or top dressing on established plants (around plants on soil surface).	Nitrogen is released quickly giving early vigorous growth, phosphate is released slowly to develop strong roots. Contains little or no K_2O.
Hoof and horn	N: 13.0 P_2O_5: 0.0 K_2O: 0.0 Trace: 0.0	On overwintered crops that need a slow long-term supply of nitrogen for leaf growth, e.g. brassicas in spring, blackcurrants.	60–120 g/sq m. Apply as base dressing several weeks before planting, or as top dressing to established plants.	Slow release nitrogen.
Bone meal	N: 3.5 P_2O_5: 20.0 K_2O: 0.0 Trace: 0.0	Source of phosphate for strawberries, fruit trees, shrubs, roses and herbaceous plants. Stimulates root growth in root crops.	120 g/sq m. Use as base dressing on established plants or in seed drills with root crops.	Always use steamed bone meal to prevent risk of human disease. Gloves can be worn as a precaution.
Worm-casts	N: 2.0 P_2O_5: 4.0 K_2O: 1.0 Trace: full range	As base or top dressing in potting compost or as a complete fertiliser. Excellent compost activator.	100 g/sq m.	Benefits soil structure, encourages soil life. Feeds soil and the plant. High beneficial bacteria content. Slightly higher K_2O when worms are fed with seaweed rather than manure.

Fertiliser	Nutrient (%)	Use	Application	Comment
Rock potash	N: 0.0 P_2O_5: 0.0 K_2O: 10.0 Trace: 0.0	Base dressing for long-term improvement of soils.	200 g/sq m.	To treat potash deficiencies, very slow release.
Rock phosphate	N: 0.0 P_2O_5: 26.0 K_2O: 0.0 Trace: 0.0	As base dressing to cure deficiencies and stimulate root growth.	200 g/sq m.	Pure ground rock for long-term improvement of soils deficient in phosphate.
Wood ash	N: 3.7 P_2O_5: 5.0 K_2O: 3.1 Trace: some	Useful addition to the compost heap.		Use young green twiggy material. Source of potassium and calcium. Essentially a 'chemical' fertiliser as the organic matter has been burnt off. Very soluble.
Seaweed meal	N: 2.8 P_2O_5: 0.2 K_2O: 2.5 Trace: full range	Base dressing or top dressing around plants and on lawns. Compost activator.	100–200 g/sq m.	An excellent supplement which feeds the soil and benefits structure. Contains many organic compounds which stimulate soil life and plant growth.
Comfrey	N: 0.02 P_2O_5: 0.03 K_2O: 0.05	As foliar spray, root dip, general tonic. Compost activator.	4.5 litres (diluted) every week on tomatoes, peppers, squash family, peas and beans.	Rot down leaves, dilute liquid extract 10–20:1. Only spray on a dull day to avoid leaf scorch. Comfrey and seaweed liquid benefit soil structure and encourage soil life. Proprietary seaweed and manure liquid sprays available.
Nettle liquid	Nettles contain more N, less K_2O and are rich in iron.			
Seaweed and liquid manures	Full range of trace elements.			

It is not yet known whether animal products can be a source of BSE, so at the present time it is advisable to wear gloves when applying these compounds.

For further details on nutrient deficiencies refer to the companion volume in this series, *Healthy Fruit and Vegetables: How to avoid diseases, disorders and deficiencies* by Pauline Pears and Bob Sherman.

Drainage

Good drainage is essential to successful soil management. Usually, excess water evaporates from the soil or through the plant (transpiration), runs off the surface, or drains through the soil to the water table or to rivers.

Sometimes you need to help water drain away. Soil structure can be destroyed by excess water. In waterlogged soil the soil life cannot breathe, root growth is restricted and nutrients cannot be made available or taken up. Fruit growth is drastically restricted in waterlogged soils.

Improving badly drained soils

- Increases the temperature.
- Improves structure.
- Improves aeration.
- Increases organic matter breakdown.
- Increases the soil life.
- Improves germination.
- Reduces disease.
- Makes nutrients more available.

The management of a badly drained soil depends on the cause.

Heavy soils

Waterlogged clay and silty soils can be improved by:

- double digging
- incorporating grit, sand, organic matter
- adding calcium-containing minerals to clays

Once improved the structure can be maintained by:

- not walking on the soil, especially when it is wet
- covering the soil surface
- creating a bed system
- ditching
- installing a drainage system

Compacted soils

These soils have a hard, solid layer under the topsoil, caused by pressure from the soil surface or a pan. The soils can become waterlogged in wet conditions and plants can suffer from drought in dry conditions because the roots cannot get through the compact layer to any water. Compaction is possible on all soil types. Indications of this include:

- puddles forming after rain
- shallow roots and stunted growth
- symptoms in profile (see page 12)
- on sandy soils, roots swell and distort when they enter the compacted layer

New houses often have compacted garden soils due to the ardent activities of the builders, but rotovating the topsoil can also lead to compaction beneath the cultivated layer.

Compaction can be relieved by:

- double digging
- increasing the depth of the topsoil
- breaking up the hard layer using a sledge hammer and heavy steel bar (brutal but satisfying)

Adding organic matter, growing deep-rooting green manures and protecting the soil surface from pressure or rain will maintain the good structure.

Compacted soil

Badly waterlogged soils

If severe waterlogging still persists, then one of the following methods may help.

Soakaway

A soakaway will take a certain amount of water but once full the problem returns.

Dig a pit of $1\,m^3$. Line with bricks, fill with stones and hard core. Cover with turves.

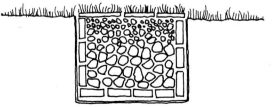

Raised beds

Raised beds increase the depth of the soil over the wet layer.

Ditches

If your land slopes and is waterlogged, then a cut-off ditch can be dug across the top of the plot to catch drainage water from higher ground. Connect this to a ditch at the bottom of the slope by ditches or tile drains.

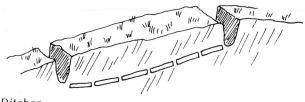

Ditches

Drainage systems

To lay a drainage system it is essential to have an outlet such as a drainage ditch. Sometimes you can run the water into public storm drains but permission from the local authority is required.

Construction

● Lay the system when the soil is just moist, to avoid further compaction.

● In a small garden use a single pipe, in a large garden a herringbone system may be required. On wet soils the arms need to be 2–3 m apart.

● Dig a trench 45 cm deep, ensuring an even, steady fall to the outlet. The drop should be not less than 33 cm in every 30 m.

● Place 15 cm of rounded stones or twiggy material in the trenches and cover with 30 cm of soil.

● Alternatively, dig a deeper trench up to 60 cm deep and 30 cm wide; place 10 cm of stones in the hole. Then lay either earthenware or plastic pipes of 50–75 mm diameter, available from agricultural merchants.

● Leave 2 mm spaces between the earthenware pipes to let the water in, and cover with slates to prevent blockage.

● Make the inner ends of arms coincide with joints in the main drain.

● Cover pipes with 10 cm of gravel and fill to the surface with topsoil.

● Check outfall for blockages periodically.

● Effective drainage systems respond quickly to rain and discharge water within a day after the beginning of a wet spell.

● A row of tile drains is sometimes required at the base of a retaining wall, where reservoirs of water can otherwise build up.

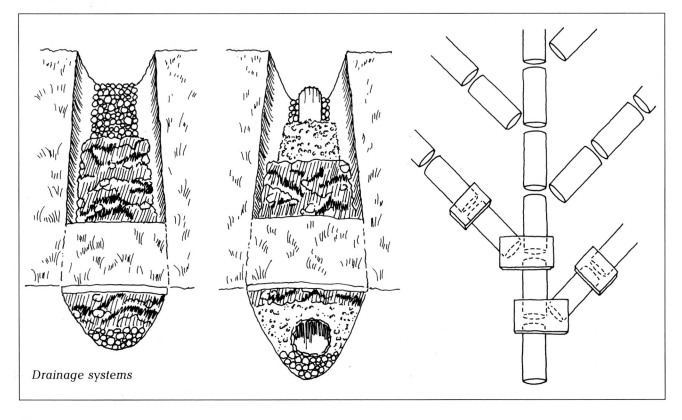

Drainage systems

Soil management at a glance

Different soil types need managing slightly differently to obtain and keep a good structure. Here is a summary to help you get the most out of your soils, whatever you start with.

Clay soils

Clays are difficult to cultivate. They are cold and heavy when wet, hard and cracked when dry. With good management, however, clays can become one of the most fertile soils.

● *Organic matter*

Can be added to surface or top few centimetres · Binds to clays, forming stable crumbs · Improves drainage, aeration and root penetration · Feeds the soil · Makes clays easier to work · Needs to be well rotted · If fresh wet material is used there are two problems: any wet clay beneath will stay wet, and the organic matter will break down without air, giving a slimy mess.

● *Cultivate*

In autumn, so frost can break up the clay · Use hand tools and avoid rotovating which compacts the subsoil.

● *Deep beds*

Can be constructed on soil that has been cultivated (to break up compaction) · Prevent further compaction and help drainage.

● *Green manures*

Dig and aerate clay soils · Remove excess water · Protect soil structure from compaction · Suitable ones include field beans, Alsike clover, mustard, grazing rye, winter tares.

● *Mulching*

Protects structure · In summer, conserves moisture and prevents drying and cracking · In winter, can keep soils warm.

● *Crops/plants*

Are planted closely to protect soil structure · For suitable crops and plants, see page 18.

● *pH*

Limes can be used on acid clays to increase pH and form soil crumbs · For alkaline or neutral clays, use gypsum to improve structure.

● *Fertility*

Clays are usually fertile if they have a good structure, and fertiliser supplements may be required only on new sites.

● *Drainage*

Good drainage of clay soils is essential · Some clay soils have small cracks and/or are over porous rocks, such as chalk or limestone, and drain well · If compacted or over impervious subsoil, then clays need drainage · This can be achieved by: double digging, breaking up compact layer with an iron bar, adding grit at two bucketfuls per sq m, making raised beds, making a soakaway, installing a drainage system.

Silty soils

The small particles of which silty soils are made can pack down easily. Also, silt cannot hold onto food like clay.

● *Organic matter*

Gives a good crumb structure and prevents packing down · Improves drainage · Feeds the soil.

● *Cultivate*

To relieve compaction · Do not walk on it.

● *Deep beds*

Improve structure where used in conjunction with green manures and organic matter · Help drainage · Prevent compaction.

● *Green manures*

Remove excess water · Aerate soil · Protect soil from compaction · Suitable ones are the same as those for clay soils.

● *Mulching*

Protects the soil structure · Prevents particles being washed down by rain · Prevents capping.

● *Crops/plants*

Maintain ground cover to protect structure · For suitable plants, see page 18.

● *pH*

Aim for a pH of between 6.5 to 7.0 to help the soil life and plants to maintain structure.

● *Fertility*

Initially, supplements may be necessary to cure deficiencies.

● *Drainage*

Can be worse in silty soils than clays because natural cracks (fissures) do not exist · Silt particles can wash down and block drainage channels · Use the same drainage methods as for clay.

Sandy soils

Sandy soils drain well, are easy to work and warm up in the spring. They support good early crops, a good rooting depth and early ripening of flowers and fruit. However, in dry weather sandy soils can suffer from drought, and in wet weather from lack of food because the water washes out the few available nutrients. Organic matter does wonders on this type of soil but for different reasons than on clays.

● *Organic matter*

Feeds the soil · Holds onto foods that would otherwise wash out · Holds water · Improves structure · Can be added to the surface because the organic matter will soon wash down through the porous soil.

● *Cultivate*

To relieve compaction · In spring, so the soil is left covered over winter.

● *Deep beds*

Are prone to capping – add organic matter and protect prepared seedbed · Use flat beds to prevent excess drainage · Prevent compaction.

● *Green manures*

Residues add organic matter/food · Prevent food washing out · Prevent erosion of soil · Suitable ones include alfalfa (deep rooting/drought resistant), buckwheat, crimson clover, bitter lupins, phacelia, grazing rye, trefoil.

● *Mulching*

Moist soils in spring, prevents drying out · In winter, prevents foods washing out.

● *Crops/plants*

Maintain plant cover to prevent leaching · For suitable plants, see page 18.

● *pH*

Sandy soils can become acid and may need liming · Check pH annually because lime is washed out by rain · Overliming is more dangerous on sandy soils than clay soils.

● *Fertility*

May need fertilisers initially, and to correct deficiencies · Regular additions of organic matter should mean fewer fertilisers are needed · Sandy soils are prone to nitrogen and potassium deficiencies.

● *Drainage*

Most sandy soils drain well and no improvement is needed · The hard layer in podsolised soils needs breaking up.

Peaty soils

Lowland peaty soils are potentially very fertile if managed correctly.

● *Organic matter*

Very little needed · In these soils the organic matter masks the effect of the minerals.

● *Cultivate*

In spring, if at all.

● *Seedbeds*

May need tamping down if there has been a winter frost.

● *Deep beds*

Are an excellent method of helping drainage on these often waterlogged soils.

● *Green manures*

Give total crop cover that reduces waterlogging · Over winter, will take out excess water · Suitable ones include field beans, Alsike clover, mustard, phacelia, grazing rye.

● *Mulching*

Moist soils in the spring, prevents drying out · If these soils dry out in hot weather, then they are difficult to rewet.

● *Crops/plants*

For suitable plants, see page 18.

● *pH*

Fen peaty soils may need some adjustment · Bog peaty soils require liming to raise the pH, to allow cultivation of a wide range of plants · Lime usually takes them to pH 5.3 · Check annually to see if the required pH has been achieved.

● *Fertility*
Some soils, particularly bog peaty soils, may need nutrient supplements to cure deficiencies · Always check pH first because acid soils may upset the nutrient uptake.

● *Drainage*
These soil types tend to become waterlogged · Deep beds assist drainage · Add grit at two bucketfuls per sq m · Make a soakaway · Install a drainage system.

Chalk and limestone soils

These soils have a natural, varied plant population. There are many plants, particularly ornamentals (calcicoles), that thrive on these alkaline soils and many that tolerate them. Growing vegetables and fruit may be more of a problem. Soft fruit which prefers slightly acid conditions may suffer from lime chlorosis (yellow/bleaching of leaves). These soils are usually thin, dry, hungry and alkaline, and require organic matter.

● *Organic matter*
Increases the depth of soil · Retains water · Lowers the pH (peat, cocopeat, grass mowings, manure) · Adds food · Add to the surface or top few centimetres · Avoid use of mushroom compost.

● *Cultivate*
Timing not crucial.

● *Deep beds*
Have advantages over soils that are dug · Increase depth of topsoil · Prevent accumulation of lime-rich runoff water.

● *Green manures*
Prevent leaching when used in conjunction with deep beds · Feed and add organic matter to the soil · Suitable ones include alfalfa, buckwheat, trefoil, grazing rye, phacelia.

● *Mulching*
Retains water · Place over moist soils in spring · Prevents leaching in winter · Protects soil from rain because these types dry into hard lumps after heavy rainfall.

● *Crops/plants*
Adjustment of pH is required before a wide range of plants can be grown · For plants that thrive and are tolerant of these soils, see page 18.

● *pH*
These soils do not need liming · For clay over chalk or limestone, use gypsum to break up the clay · Occasionally, in areas of high rainfall, the calcium carbonate is washed down giving a thin acid layer above the chalk or limestone · Bring up calcium with deep-rooting crops and green manures.

● *Fertility*
Nutrient deficiencies are usually due to the alkalinity of the soil.

● *Drainage*
Not usually needed because these soils are very porous · If clay is found over the chalk, then add grit or organic matter to help drainage.

Loamy soils

These soils contain a good mixture of sand, silt and clay, and if cared for, then they can give excellent crop yields.

● *Organic matter*
Maintains good soil structure · Feeds the soil.

● *Cultivate*
If there is any compaction.

● *Deep beds*
Can maintain a good structure on these soils · Can be raised or flat.

● *Green manures*
Improve and maintain soil structure · Feed the soil · Keep nutrients in the top few centimetres.

● *Mulching*
Protects structure.

● *Crops/plants*
Plant closely to protect structure · These soils support a wide range of crops, depending on their pH.

● *pH*
Test pH and lime if necessary.

● *Fertility*
Use supplementary fertilisers if the plants show signs of deficiency.

● *Drainage*
Take measures to improve drainage if required.

Soil problems at a glance

Problem	Symptoms	Cause	Cure
Waterlogging	Poor root growth. Stunted plants. Few worms. Grey mottling in profile. Smell of bad eggs. Over winter plants turn yellow and collapse. Rain puddles on surface. Indicator weeds: horsetail, coltsfoot, silverweed, cinquefoil.	Compacted soil. Heavy soil (silt/clay). Peaty soil. Pan in subsoil. High water table. High rainfall.	Double dig. Add organic matter (not to peaty soils), grit, sand. Create raised beds. Maintain ground cover with plants to remove water and prevent further compaction. Use hollow-tine fork to aerate lawn. Build a soakaway. Dig drains. Install drainage system.
Dry soil	Shrivelled plants. Poor growth. Cracks in soil.	Sandy soil. Shallow soil over chalk and limestone.	Add organic matter. Use flat beds. Maintain soil cover using deep-rooting species to bring up water. Mulch the soil when moist to conserve water. Irrigate but prevent loss by mulching.
Nutrient imbalance (1)	Reduced growth. Yellow leaves (especially older ones). Leguminous weeds.	Lack of nitrogen due to deficiency or acid soil. Nutrients being washed out by rain. Waterlogged soil. Dry soil.	Add compost, manure. Add supplements, such as blood, fish and bone, hoof and horn. Use nettle sprays. Grow legumes. Dig in sappy green manures. Mulch soil and grow green manures to prevent leaching. Lime acid soils. Rotate crops to balance ones which feed the soil with ones that remove a lot of nitrogen.
Nutrient imbalance (2)	Older leaves dark and dull. Red streaks in sweetcorn and fat hen. Small roots.	Phosphate deficiency caused by acid soil, deficiency in soil minerals, or very alkaline soil.	Add organic matter. Add supplements, such as blood, fish and bone, bone meal. Add compost to stimulate soil life. Lime acid soils. Add acidic manures to alkaline soils.
Nutrient imbalance (3)	Yellowing leaves, scorched at edges. Poor roots, fruiting and flowering. More susceptible to pests and diseases (e.g. chocolate spot on broad beans).	Potash deficiency caused by leaching in well-drained soil, too much nitrogen or phosphate, or very acid or alkaline soil.	Add organic matter. Mulch and grow green manures to prevent leaching. Adjust pH if necessary.
Nutrient imbalance (4)	Stunted growth. Curled, distorted leaves with black spots. Stem and root tips brown. Fruit: tomatoes get blossom end rot and apples get bitter pit. Undecayed organic matter accumulates as soil life dies.	Calcium deficiency. Acid soil. Peaty soil. High rainfall.	Lime, after checking the pH to make sure it is not a disease.
Nutrient imbalance (5)	Yellowing between veins, symptoms in old leaves first.	Magnesium deficiency in acid soil, in soil with high rainfall, or caused by too much potassium.	Add organic matter. Add dolomite lime. Mulch and sow green manures to prevent food washing out.
Nutrient imbalance (6)	Wide range of symptoms in plants.	Trace element deficiency caused by very alkaline soil or overfertilisation.	Add organic matter which contains trace elements. Sow green manures to recycle mulch. Use seaweed, calcified seaweed, worm-casts. Adjust soil pH if necessary.
Capping	Thin hard crust on bare soil.	Heavy rain on seedbed. More likely on sandy and silty soils.	Add organic matter. Protect seedbed. Cover seeds with compost rather than soil.

Shallow soil	Restricted plant roots. In a drought, hot spots of yellowing plants mark the shallow soil.	*Location*: Shallow soils are common on brows and slopes, on hard rocks and in the uplands.	Add organic matter. Make deep beds/mounds. Grow green manures. *Mulch*: Shallow soils on high ground usually get plenty of water and need mulches to prevent foods washing out. Shallow soils on low ground are more prone to drought and need mulching when moist to conserve moisture.
Stony soil	Large rocks in soil.		Add organic matter. Make deep beds/mounds. Grow green manures. Some calcareous soils are very stony: do not remove them all (an impossible task) but leave some as a mulch to conserve moisture in these free-draining soils.
Acid soil	Plants have stunted growth. Some have mottled leaves. Split fruits. Pimples on trees! Brassicas prone to club root.	The disease-like symptoms are caused by nutrient imbalances, due to the acid soil.	Lime in soil. Use mushroom compost.
Alkaline soil	Plants have stunted growth. Bleached leaves. Potatoes prone to scab.	The disease-like symptoms are caused by nutrient imbalances, due to the alkaline soil.	Lower the soil pH by adding acidic organic compost and manures.
Soil heavy to work	Soil sticks to spade and fork.	Clay soil or silty soil.	Improve structure by adding organic matter. Double dig to break up any compaction; hard work, but well worth it in the end. Make deep beds. Sow green manures to dig soil. Maintain crop cover to protect structure using suitable rotations and mulches. Add lime (if acid) or gypsum (if neutral/alkaline).
Coastal	Poor growth. Wind-swept, scorched plants.	Salt spray. High winds.	Grow plants of a maritime origin. Add organic matter. Create a windbreak to keep off high winds and salt spray.
Compaction	Poor growth. Few worms. Stunted shallow roots. Occurs on all soil types. Same symptoms as waterlogging when wet or drought when dry because roots cannot get through compact layer to water.	Pressure on the soil from feet, machinery or rain. Some pans caused by soluble salts precipitating out between topsoil and subsoil (podsol).	Break up compact layer. Create deep beds. Prevent further compaction by adding organic matter or growing green manures. Protect surface with a mulch, green manure or crop cover.
Very sandy soil	Poor germination. Poor growth. Lack of water. Lack of nutrients.	Large spaces between particles. Similar symptoms found on all soil types after frost where the soil has 'heaved' up.	Add organic matter to create soil crumbs and small pores for water. Mulch with organic matter. Grow green manures. Consolidate and add organic matter to frost-heaved beds.
No soil	Poor growth.	Gardens around a new home where the topsoil has been removed or buried deeply. As for shallow soil.	Add organic matter. Mulch with organic matter. Grow green manures. Use deep beds. Patience!
Contaminated soil	e.g. urban lead pollution.	Most lead pollution is airborne and can be washed off vegetables with a weak solution of vinegar.	Add organic matter, as less lead is transferred to vegetables in soils treated in this way. For soils contaminated with pesticides or heavy metals, seek advice from experts, such as HDRA, the Soil Association or a local agricultural advisory body.

Glossary

Actinomycete: a type of bacteria resembling a fungus.

Alluvial deposits: minerals and soils deposited by water.

Autotrophic bacteria: bacteria that make their food from inorganic material.

Base dressing: fertiliser applied immediately before sowing or planting.

Brassicas: cabbages, Brussels sprouts, cauliflowers, kale, turnips, swedes, cress, salad, rape and mustards. All are closely related and are members of the 'Brassica' family of plants.

Calcareous: containing carbonate of lime.

Cap: a hard crust on the soil surface.

Cations: positively charged particles.

Colloid: a substance that disperses into fine particles in solution but does not quite dissolve.

Compaction: where soil is packed down due to weight from above.

Double digging: cultivating the soil to a depth of two spits (a spit is the depth of a spade).

Drill: a narrow, shallow depression made in the soil, by the edge of a rake or other tool, for sowing seed into.

Fossil fuel: a fuel derived from decomposed plants and animals, e.g. coal and oil.

Friable: describes a fine, crumbly soil with no hard or wet lumps.

Gley: a waterlogged soil, usually over clay.

Green manure: a crop that is grown to incorporate into the soil.

Gypsum: calcium sulphate, used to break up clay soils that do not need liming.

Humus: a formless, black, jelly-like substance containing a wide range of complex life chemicals. The main breakdown product of organic matter.

Leaching: the removal of soluble minerals from the soil by water draining through it.

Leaf mould: decomposed leaves.

Legumes: peas, beans, clover and other related crops.

Lime: a powder formed by crushing or processing limestone rock. Lime makes soil and compost more alkaline.

Loam: a fertile soil with balanced proportions of clay, silt and sand.

Mulch: any material spread over the soil.

Mycorrhiza: a beneficial association between a fungus and the roots of a plant.

Nitrogen fixer: the air is full of nitrogen and some bacteria, known as nitrogen fixers, are able to take it up. Plants such as peas and beans have these bacteria living in their roots, and can use the nitrogen that the bacteria extract from the air.

No-dig system: a system of growing that avoids any turning over of the soil.

Organic: a method of growing plants which avoids the use of chemical pesticides and artificial fertilisers.

Organic matter: composed of the remains of dead plants and animals.

Overwinter: survive the winter.

Pan: a hard layer below the soil surface, often only 30 cm to 45 cm below the surface.

pH: a measure of the acidity of the soil. A pH of 7 is taken to be neutral; a soil with a pH of less than 7 is said to be acid, while a pH figure of more than 7 is said to be alkaline.

Photosynthesis: the process by which a green plant is able to make carbohydrates from water and carbon dioxide, using light as an energy source and chlorophyll to absorb the light.

Plant nutrient: any of the mineral substances that are absorbed by the roots of plants for nourishment.

Podsol: an acid, infertile soil found in regions of heavy rainfall and long cool winters.

Puffy bed: a loose soil full of air, usually arising after frost action.

Tilth: a fine, crumbly surface layer of soil.

Top dressing: fertiliser applied onto the soil around a plant.

Trace elements: food materials required by plants in very small amounts only.

Transpiration: the continual loss of water vapour from leaves and stems.

Water table: the level in the soil below which the soil is saturated by ground water.

Index Chapter headings are in bold type.

48